PROCUREMENT AND SUPPLY CHAIN MANAGEMENT IN PROJECTS

Dr. Evans Vidija Sagwa, PhD

ISBN:1532786409
ISBN-13:9781532786402

DEDICATION

Dedicated to Hilder Alivitsa Kisame.

CONTENTS

ACKNOWLEDGMENTS

I wish to acknowledge my indebtedness to all professors, lecturers and teachers under whom I have had a privilege to undertake my studies, my students at certificate, diploma, and higher diploma, undergraduate and post graduate levels. I am also indebted to managers and practitioners who have participated in seminars and workshops that I have facilitated over the years. In the years I have been a student, researcher, employee, lecturer and administrator, I have gathered useful resources and experiences in the management field. I am grateful that Amazon Publishers agreed to publish this book.

I am greatly indebted to all authors of the books, session papers, manuals, policy guidelines, legal documents and other reference materials. To my family, I owe them an immeasurable debt for their unceasing support that has been a source of inspiration over the years.

CHAPTER 1

INTRODUCTION

Definition of procurement and supply chain management

Procurement refers to the aspect of project management related to retaining goods and services from outside a company or an entity. Procurement is an area into which a project manager has to give an input in most organizations. The project manager usually does not have the authority to enter into contracts on behalf of the company and is usually not asked to administer or enter into binding or administration of a contract once they are in place. A project manager needs to have a working knowledge of procurement.

Supply Chain Management (SCM) is the oversight of material, information and finances as they move in a process from suppliers to manufacturer to wholesalers to retailer to the consumer. Supply chain involves co-coordinating and integrating these flows both within and among companies. It is argued that the ultimate goal of any effective supply chain management system is to reduce inventory (with the assumption that products are available when needed). As a way of providing solutions for successful supply chain management, sophisticated software systems that have interfaces and web based application, service providers have to combine efforts to provide some of the solutions needed in supply chain

1

management services for organizations.

Logistics management is that part of supply chain management that plans, implements and controls the efficient, effective forward and reverse flow and storage of goods, services and related information between the point of origin and the point of consumption in order to meet the customers' requirements.

Need for supply chain management

Supply chain management is the systematic and strategic co-ordination management for supplying goods, products and services that are acquired by the end customer. The need or importance of supply chain management includes:

1. Creation of net value.
2. Building competitive infrastructure.
3. Synchronizing the supply of goods/services.
4. Measuring performance on global standards
5. Leveraging on worldwide logistics.
6. Reduction of inventory costs.
7. Provision of a better medium for sharing of information among stakeholders.
8. Improvement of customer satisfaction.
9. Increase in cash flow.
10. Improved quality of products or services.
11. Improvement in profit through a reduction in the use of fixed assets in the supply chain.

Concept of project procurement

The concept of project procurement usually involves a systematic process of identifying an appropriate supplier and procuring through purchase or acquisition of the necessary project services, goods or results from outside suppliers or vendors who will carry out the work. This is usually a function undertaken by the project manager. The underlying fact if most entities, the project manager need to understand the basis of procurement management. The responsibility of procurement for the project is usually shared between the project manager and the procurement department. The project manager has to provide requirements to the procurement specialists in order to make sure that the right supplier is chosen. The procurement specialist in turn provides guidance to the project manager on how to manage the vendor or suppliers relationships successfully.

There are six processes that are widely recognized in the project management industry as integral to project procurement management:

1. **Planning purchases and acquisitions**

   This is the process of determining the items to purchase for the project and when they are needed. This process is typically under the control of the project manager, given that centralized purchasing department may not know what each particular project team needs to execute their project.

   During this step needs that require outsourcing are identified. The sources for obtaining the required services, goods or outcomes/results are differentiated through a comprehensive market analysis. While planning the procurement, project objectives are reviewed to ensure that the acquisition does not deviate from the stated objectives. This step of planning purchases and acquisitions also involves identification of the resources that are necessary for the acquisition, determination of the contract type needed to secure the acquisition, and preparation of a procurement management plan.

2. **Contract planning**

   This is the process of creating requirements for all the products and services that the project team needs. This process or step has to be performed by the project management team. In contract planning, it is necessary for the project team to provide the detailed item or services descriptions that they will require. The requests for proposals and bids have to be well documented to avoid challenges that are associated with poorly documented requests for proposals.

3

During this stage/step of contract planning the project manager needs to start identifying potential companies that can supply the products or services.

3. Requesting seller/supplier responses

During this stage / step, sellers' responses are requested. Vendors or suppliers are requested to provide information regarding their capabilities and capacity to provide anticipated services or products, through quotations. The project team may perform some tasks on this process. This process is typically owned by the purchasing function/department. specific vendors or suppliers who may be selected or identified are usually placed on a pre-qualified supplier list.

4. Selecting suppliers

Selection of suppliers is a process that is associated with the actual choosing of the supplier who will actually provide the product or service. Once the prospective suppliers have been selected (pre-qualified), their bids or proposals to supply are evaluated so as to determine the best supplier who may be awarded the contract to deliver the goods or services. The project team may make the final selection. Usually this process is managed by the purchasing department. After the supplier is chosen, the contract is negotiated. The purchasing department generally signs the final contract. Most organizations are usually reluctant to allow project managers to enter into legal contractual relationships.

5. Contract administration

This is the process of managing the relationship with the contracted company vendor or supplier. The project manager usually works on a day to day basis with the suppliers account manager. Administration of contracts is very critical to project procurement activities. Obligations, responsibilities and performance goals need to be outlined clearly, for satisfactory performance of a project. Performance monitoring, evaluation and review by the project manager has done to obtain desired results. It is important to control and clearly document any contract changes or adjustments so as to prevent un warranted legal claims.

6. Contract closure

The final step/stage in the project procurement management process is the contract closure. This usually occurs if the contractual relationship existed only for the life of the project. The contract comes to an end when the project is over. The contract is audited to make sure that all terms of the contract have been fulfilled. Contract closure involves evaluating the performance of the supplier or vendor and documenting the lessons that have been acquired while executing the contract. The project team is usually involved by the purchasing department or function to make sure that all the contracted work has been completed and to obtain feedback about the supplier relationship.

Project management skills and procurement management

It should be noted that each project is unique and may require a set of project management skills that may vary from project to project. These project management skills have to be developed by a project manager for the success of project procurement management. Some of the key project management skills that should be developed by a project manager include;

i) Leadership and management skills

The project manager has to possess leadership skills to be able to provide visionary guidance and inspiration to those that they are guiding, management skills can greatly assist a project manager to accomplish tasks and get work done through others. These skills are crucial in procurement management since some of the areas being carried out in a project may be new, hence a project manager may need to be innovative in obtaining goods or services needed to achieve project goals.

i)Terms builder and team leader

Team building and team leadership skills are desirable soft skills that project managers must concentrate more often, the project manager will be expected to bring together stakeholders who have not worked together like employees from various department, suppliers, vendors, government officers etc who have to work on one project. The project manager has to play the role of team leader in order to tap the team synergy (2+2=5) for the realization of project objectives. This will contribute to adherence to agreements and procurement schedules as set out in the project.

ii)Excellent communication skills

Excellent communication skills are crucial in project management. The project manager has to ensure that all communication is effective, appropriate and complete. This will ensure that all stakeholders in a project including vendors/suppliers are updated and perform their tasks and honour their part of the contract that they are expected to fulfill in relation to project procurement management process.

iii)Good organizer

The project manager has to cultivate good organization skills. This will ensure that all structures and systems are formulated and put in place to facilitate the implementation of project plans. The project manager has to ensure that all the stakeholders in the procurement process are well briefed regarding their roles and responsibilities. The project manager has to ensure that all aspects of the project are well documented and executed. This will go a long way in ensuring that all aspects including delivery of goods and services are done on time and all acquisitions are accomplished for the success of the project.

iv) Competent and consistent planner

Possession of appropriate competencies and consistent planning skills are key project management skills. A project manager should have the ability to develop proactive plans that have alternative courses of action. This will ensure that challenges that are encountered in the life of a project are overcome. In case of suppliers, if one supplier is not able to deliver on contracts for suppliers, appropriate planning can see a project being completed with suppliers from alternative suppliers at short notice.

v) Problem solving skills

Due to the nature of projects, many processes and people are involved. Challenges and problems are normally encountered in project implementation. The project manager has to develop problem solving skills that would assist in resolving conflicts between specialist groups, individuals, sections, vendors or suppliers. These problem solving skills ensure that when conflicts arise, they are resolved at the earliest opportunity for the project to remain on course and mutual management in the course of project procurement management.

vi) Negotiation and influencing skills

The project manager has to build strong negotiation and influencing skills. More often, the timelines, schedules, quantities, quality specifications among other aspects as indicated in projects have to be negotiated. This may occasioned by some circumstances or events that could not have been factored in at the time of project formulation. The project manager will be expected to influence other stakeholders to buy into the adjusted schedules.

vii) Budget formulation and budget management skills

Projects are expected to be implemented within some self budgets. The project manager has to develop superior budget formulation and budget management skills to be able to align the procurement plan to the allocated budget in order to realize success in the project being undertaken. Hence the significance of budget management skills to ensure that procurement is managed within the allocated budget to guarantee project success.

Project manager's role in the procurement process

The role that will be played by the project manager in a procurement process will be influenced by the type of project being handled, terms of reference and the policy adopted by an organization with reference to project management. It is generally taken that issues relating to procurement will be handled by the procurement function or department in an organization. However, the project manager will be expected to facilitate and play a crucial role in procurement of goods and services relating to a project being managed by the project manager. The role of the project manager in the procurement process includes;

i) Procurement documents

The project manager and his/her project teams are expected to participate fully in the preparation of procurement documents. This will include provision of technical details that pertain to the projects, services and outcomes expected from the suppliers or vendors.

ii) Scope of work

The project manager is expected to provide the statement of work that the project is expected to cover. This forms the basis of engaging the suppliers or vendors.

iii) Staffing

The project manager has to play a crucial role in the preparation of duties and responsibilities that internal and external staff should be assigned. Given that the project manager understands what results need to be procured and the specific stages or phases that staff will be needed. This goes a long way in helping to recruit or outsource the necessary staff with relevant skills and competencies.

iv)Schedules

The project manager plays a key role in drawing up schedules for the receiving of goods or supplies. The project manager and the project management team also liaise with the vendors or suppliers to ensure that the appropriate project components are delivered as per the agreed schedules.

v)Costs

The project manager participates in the analysis and review of costs related to the project activities. This helps in ensuring that materials, supplies and services are procured at cost effective rakes to facilitate the successful completion of the project.

vi)Performance reports

The project manager provides performance reports regarding the vendors or suppliers in the course of the project. These reports may provide valuable information regarding the suitability of the supplier. In some instances, the supplier may be provided with a sample task to perform. Based on the report provided by the project manager, the supplier may then be awarded the complete task to perform in the case of a favorable report by the project manager.

vii)Changes / adjustments

It might be desirable to make some changes or adjustments on an on-going project. The project manager has to communicate this kind of changes to all the stakeholders on a given project. These changes or adjustments may have implications on the procurement aspects of the project.

viii) Deliverables

The project manager and the project team play a major role in the inspection of deliverables provided by the supplier or vendor. This inspection is done with a view of verifying compliance and quality standards.

ix) Payments

The project manager and the project team have to endorse the delivery notes; goods received notes, quality reports and invoices to facilitate payments to be made for goods and services rendered to a project by the vendors or suppliers.

x) Procurement audit

The project manager has to take part in the preparation of an audit report for the procurement aspects of the project. This report among other things rates the performance of all the vendors or suppliers, taking note of the achievements, challenges, lessons learnt and suggestions on areas that require improvement.

Procurement Functions and Project Success

The ways through which the procurement function adds value to project success include:

i) Ensuring timely delivery of procured goods or services to ensure that the project is completed on schedule.

ii) Adherence to quality specifications and standards. This ensures that work is completed to the highest level of quality.

iii) Obtaining of the products or services for the project at competitive prices. The procurement function can add value to the project success through competitive prices to facilitate completion of the project within the set budget for the project.

iv) The procurement function through proactive measures can ensure that stringent standards are set for adherence to quality and packaging specifications. This helps in machine loading and avoidance of change over times that lead to operation or loss of production time. This enhances project success.

v) The procurement function has to ensure that orders that are placed clearly indicate the place that the goods or services have to be delivered. This promptly minimizes the post-order lead times. Once products or materials are delivered in the right place, this enhances productivity and project success.

Best practices in procurement

Organizations are aspiring to be the best in their areas of operation the modern dynamic business environment of today. In order to achieve this aspiration, firms need to embrace best practices in procurement, given that procurement activities and inventory may hold a substantial amount of the operating capital that a firm or organization may have.

Some of the best practices in procurement may include:

a) Effective alignment of supply chain organization and staff in an entity.
b) Adoption of appropriate technology in supply chain and procurement tasks/activities.
c) Establishment of an alliance with key stakeholders like suppliers or vendors.
d) Engaging in collaborative strategic sourcing.
e) Focusing on total cost of ownership and not just price. This may involve carrying out a life cycle cost analysis in projects.
f) Managing contracts under the supply chain function in an organization.
g) Making optimum use of company owned inventory.
h) Establishing appropriate levels of control.
i) Emphasizing on green initiatives and corporate social responsibility.
j) Carrying out a Cost Benefit Analysis (CBA) or sometimes referred to as Benefit- Cost Analysis (BCA) this is the systematic process for calculating and comparing benefits and costs of a project.
k) Value improvements – This is the practice of enhancing the value of a project by engaging in practices that assist in cutting costs to increase the rate of return on investment on a project.

CHAPTER 2
SUPPLY CHAIN MANAGEMENT: STORAGE AND WAREHOUSING

Definition of Storage and Warehousing

Storage is the holding of stock between the time of production and final consumption.

A warehouse denotes an establishment for storage and accumulation of goods. A warehouse is an arrangement by which goods are stored when they are not immediately needed and are kept in such a manner that they are protected from deterioration. A warehouse is a commercial building for storage of goods used by manufacturers, importers, exporters, wholesalers, transport businesses, customers etc. warehouses usually have loading docks, to load and unload goods from tracks. At times warehouses may be designed for loading goods directly from railways, airports, or seaports. Warehouses often have cranes and forklifts for moving goods which are usually placed on pallets and loaded into pallet racks. Warehousing is one of the main spheres of logistics.

Storage and warehousing

The broad meaning of storage and warehousing is the keeping of finished goods or materials (raw, packing, components) for manufacturing, agriculture or commercial purposes. Warehousing contains numerous functions like acceptance of products (loading, unloading), inspection, and proper storage, that is, the warehouse management system which includes warehouse infrastructure, tracking systems and communication between product stations.

Need for storage and warehousing

The need for storage and warehousing can be explained by the following factors:

i) The time gap between the production of goods and their final consumption.

ii) Organizations often engage in large scale or mass production. This require storage and warehousing to store large quantities of raw materials, packaging, work in progress and finished stock to ensure steady or smooth and continuous production.

iii) The production that is done may be for anticipated future demand and not for immediate sale. This makes it necessary to store goods to be sold off at a future date.

iv) Some goods or products may be produced throughout the year yet, their demand is seasonal. In such cases, storage and warehousing is crucial to ensure that the goods or products are available when demanded.

v) Certain goods are usually stored for seasoning purposes to enhance their quality or for better task and flavour, for example wine. Wines are not consumed immediately they are made. Their taste and flavour is enhanced after storage and preservation for a given duration of time.

vi) Some goods may be demanded throughout the year but their production is seasonal. These kinds of goods may be stored so that they are made available throughout the year.

vii) The storage and warehousing process can facilitate the distribution of goods from the production centre to the market.

viii) Storage and warehousing of goods can be done with a speculative intention of earning more profit.

Types of warehouses

The types of warehouses include:

i)Public warehouse

This type of a warehouse is operated in accordance with the law for the purpose of storage of goods for other people or the public at a profit. It provides facilities for storing all kinds of goods.

ii)Private warehouse

This is a warehouse that belongs to the owner of the goods, usually a wholesaler. This enables the wholesaler to supply these goods to the retailers at a future date or when they need the goods. Private warehouses enable the owners of the goods to store them in order to meet their respective needs.

iii)Bonded warehouses

This is a warehouse which is licensed to accept imported goods for storage before payment of customs duties. By storing the goods in a bounded warehouse, the importer gains some control over the goods without paying duty. The goods in bonded warehouses are usually put under the strict supervision of customs officers.

iv)Government warehouse

These types of warehouses are mainly located at important sea ports and in most cases are owned by the dock authorities. The general public can also use these types of warehouses on the payment of prescribed charges. Where a customer is not able to pay the charges by a given time, the goods can be disposed off to defray the charges or rent that was to be paid by the customer.

Basic Philosophy of Good Warehouse Management

Those who are entrusted with the responsibility of managing a warehouse have to take all precautions to ensure that the warehouse efficiently and effectively achieves its set objectives. The warehouse manager has to play the assigned part effectively. The warehouse functions have to be clearly spelt out. The warehouse activities may be centralized or decentralized to suit the desired requirements. The warehouse management operations have to be evaluated on an ongoing basis and appropriate intervention measures taken.

Role of Warehouse Manager

Depending on the type and nature of a warehouse, the roles that may be handled by a warehouse manager include;

i) Keeping track of all the goods/items that come into and out of the warehouse.

ii) Keeping an account of detailed paper trait regarding warehouse activities.

iii) The warehouse manager should be well aware of the inventory levels.

iv) Should be aware of costs involved in purchasing new products.

v) Has to keep track of organizational resources like equipment and vehicles.

vi) Has a responsibility for warehouse staff and personnel deployed to the warehouse.

vii) Maintenance of equipment and warehouse facilities.

viii) Responsible for the safety and security aspects in the warehouse.

Warehouse Functions

The basic warehouse objectives and functions are;

1. Receiving of goods into the warehouse.
2. Identification and sorting of goods that are brought to the warehouse.
3. Dispatching of goods for storage. This involves moving of received goods from the inbound are to the storage area.

4. Placing of goods into storage within the stores layout and the appropriate storage equipment.
5. Storage of goods which is the traditional role of a warehouse.
6. Retrieval of goods from storage for outward bound process.
7. Order accumulation- this is putting together the orders that need to be serviced by the warehouse.
8. Packing – the goods may require grading, branding or packaging before they are removed from the warehouse.
9. Shipping or dispatching of goods via the appropriate means may also be handled by a warehouse.
10. Information management – the warehouse maintains records and keeps track of information regarding goods that are delivered to the warehouse, stored, shipped or moved out of the warehouse.
11. Protection of goods from damage, deterioration, heat, dust moisture etc. the warehouse management has to make special arrangements depending on the nature of the goods.
12. Risk bearing – the warehouse has to bear the risk for the value in the goods until they are removed from the warehouse.
13. Processing – some of the goods that are kept in a warehouse may need processing e.g. bananas may need ripening, timber may need seasoning etc.

Centralization and Decentralization of Warehouse Management

Depending on the needs of a given organization, warehouse and inventory management activities may be centralized or decentralized.

Centralization of Warehouse Management

Warehouse and inventory management activities are said to be centralized when the decision making authority is vested in one centre within the organization or entity.

Advantages of Centralization of Warehouse Management

i. A total or companywide view can be taken on aspects regarding warehousing.
ii. This is a much stronger warehouse management system.

iii. More professional inventory and warehouse managers can be attracted and retained.

iv. An organization can be able to access special buying opportunities e.g. bulk buying.

v. Economies of scale can be enjoyed in many aspects of inventory and warehousing management like security, personnel, logistics and risk management.

Disadvantages of Centralization of Warehouse Management

i. Those who manage a centralized inventory and warehouse management system may lack knowledge of local events.

ii. Those in the units or user points feel that they are disenfranchised in terms of local opportunities.

iii. The system may consume a lot of time as respective users liaise with the centre regarding their requirements.

iv. In case of shortfalls in quality or inability to meet delivery times, the users in the units cannot be held accountable or responsible.

v. When challenges are experienced at the centre, this may adversely affect all units.

Decentralization of Warehouse Management

Warehouse and inventory management activities are said to be decentralized when the users are delegated with authority to make their warehouse and inventory decisions.

Advantages of Decentralization of Warehouse Management

i. The users can be able to use their knowledge of local activities to make prudent decisions.

ii. The user can be able to take advantage of local networking opportunities.

iii. The users can be aware of unique conditions to the advantage of the organization.

iv. It enhances the local management control by the users.

v.   This process provides the units with a sense of ownership of the process.

Disadvantages of decentralization of Warehouse Management

i.   The local inventory management team may lack inventory management skills.

ii.   Decentralized inventory and warehouse management structures usually have a bias for high inventories.

iii.   There is a tendency to over react on events or activities that maybe temporary or transient in nature.

iv.   Due to the scale of operation, decentralized systems may not be able to enjoy economies of large scale activities that may be associated with bulk purchases and operations.

v.   This may lead to duplication of activities across the various warehouses in the same organization on inventory and warehouse management activities/functions.

Evaluation of Warehouse Operations

It is important to evaluate or assess or appraise the warehouse operations to ensure that an organization saves money and resources while achieving the objectives for which a warehouse is set out to achieve. The strategies or ways through which warehouse operations can be evaluated include:

i.   Evaluation of the utilization of the storage space available in the workplace.

ii.   Assessment of critical inventory levels for each product that is kept in the warehouse.

iii.   Assessment of the stock pickers' time. This may require that fast moving products are kept in close proximity to save on stock pickers' time.

iv.   The level and use of technology in the warehouse, for instance, are bar codes used to track the availability and storage of products in the warehouse.

v.   An assessment of the ability of expanding storage space e.g. through appropriate layout or equipment.

vi.   An assessment of product location can be done to find out whether proper zoning or colour codes have been used.,

vii.   An evaluation of the warehouse staff in terms of their knowledge regarding stock and their location.

viii.   An evaluation of the packaging that has been done by the vendors, whether it is appropriate or costs have to be incurred to store or package for dispatch.

ix.   An assessment of the level of safety and security maintained in the warehouse and preparedness in case of emergencies or disasters.

x.   Accessibility of the warehouse.

Storage Equipment and Methods

The kind of storage equipment and methods used in handling and storage of goods in a warehouse affect the efficiency and effectiveness of warehouse operations. Storage equipment is used for holding or buffering materials over a period of time. Storage equipment and methods include;

1. Block stacking
2. Selective Pallet Rack
3. Drive Through Rack
4. Drive in Rack
5. Flow Through Rack
6. Push Through Rack
7. Sliding Rack
8. Stacking Frame
9. Cantilever
10. Shelves
11. Bins
12. Storage Carousel
13. Automation Storage/Retrieval System
14. Split Case Order Picking System
15. Mezzanine

Benefits of Storage Equipment and Methods

The benefits that are associated with storage equipments and methods include;

1. Reduction of material holding costs.
2. Optimum utilization of floor space.
3. Ergonomic considerations that enhance the safety of employees which boosts staff productivity.
4. Easy location of materials.
5. Effective management of inventory to eliminate stock outs and streamlining of inventory levels.
6. Increase stock picking accuracy.

The storage of goods with appropriate equipment like cold rooms, refrigeration or controlled temperatures assist in the preservation and protection of stored goods or items.

CHAPTER 3

INVENTORY MANAGEMENT

Effective inventory management is concerned with knowing what an organization has, where it is in use, and how much finished products have been produced. Inventory management is the process of efficiently supervising the constant flow of items into and out of an existing inventory. The inventory management process usually involves controlling the transfer of items into an organization in order to prevent the inventory from becoming too high or reducing to levels that can adversely affect the operations of the organization.

Inventory management can be defined as, the overseeing and controlling of the ordering, storage and use of components that a company will use in the production of the items it will sell as well as the overseeing and controlling of finished products for sale. It should be noted that the inventory of a business is one of its major assets and represents an investment that is filed up until the item is sold or used in the production of an item that is sold. It costs an organization money to hold inventory, keep track and insure inventories. A good inventory management system creates a purchasing plan that help in ensuring that items are available when they required eg through Just-In-Time(JIT) method. The procurement system also keeps tracks of existing inventory and how it is being used.

Inventory Control

Inventory control is a strong management tool that helps an organization to reduce its cost of doing business or operating. The objectives of inventory control include:

i. Providing an assurance that inventories or materials will be available when they are required.
ii. Helps an organization to procure its input or materials through economic buying, which reduces the procurement cost to the minimum.
iii. Helps in avoiding the likely shortage of materials.
iv. Avoidance of overstocking of materials.
v. Reduction of inventory carry cost
vi. Provides the purchasing unit with the flexibility of choosing how to purchase to take advantage of quantity discounts, forward buying, adjustment unit of quantities to buy etc.

Classification of Purchases

These are a variety of classification systems that can be used to assist in inventory control and in deciding the quantity of inventory that should be held at a given time.

These classification systems may include the following:

i. The inventory can be classified according to the type of requirements like energy, raw materials, parts and sub assemblies, Materials for Repairs and Operations (MROs) items, resale items, packaging materials, tools and capital goods.
ii. Inventory can be classified in terms of the frequency with which the items are purchased. Some items that are in most cases of a capital nature are obtained or acquired infrequently or rarely. Some other types of inventory may be bought on a repetitive basis. An organization may adopt a different way of acquiring capital items or inventory.

iii.   Inventory or items may be classified in terms of whether or not purchases are for the purpose of stock replenishment. It is mostly assumed that most stock items or inventory are bright as repetitive purchases, as a result there may be a risk of purchasing too much stock or inventory for the non-repetitive purchase.

iv.   Inventory or items can be classified based on the physical or chemical nature and dimension of the purchased items. Such requirements or items may be solids, liquids, or gases. Some of these items may be perishable, hazardous etc. The nature of packaging, size and shape of the package can differentiate the inventory.

v.   Inventory or items can also be classified based on the type of transport, items that are packaged in smaller quantities can be transported on tracks, liquid inventory may be moved through a pipeline, container may be used to transport bulky items, other kinds of inventory may be moved through air freight etc.

vi.   Inventory can be classified in terms of its destination, some items may be destined to customers outside an organization and some items may be purchased for internal use within an organization. This kind of classification can be identified as external or internal requirements.

vii. Items or inventory may be classified based on monetary value. An Italian by name Vilfredo Pareto made an observation that regardless of the country, a small portion of the population controlled most wealth. This observation led to the Pareto curve whose general principles hold in a wide range of situations. In inventory management, the Pareto curve usually holds for items purchased, number of suppliers, items held in inventory and many other aspects. The Pareto curve is often referred to as the 80-20 rule or more usefully ABC analysis which results in three classes or classifications A, B and C.

Class	Percent of Total Items Purchased	Percent of Total Purchase Shillings
A Items	10	70-80
B Items	10-20	10-15
C Items	70-80	10-20

It should be noted that these percentages may vary from entity to entity and organizations may use more classes of materials. The principle of separation is very powerful in inventory management because it allows concentration of management efforts in the areas of highest payoff.

Stock Control and Inventory

Stock control which is also referred to as inventory control is a term that is used to indicate the quantity of stock that an organization has at any one time and how the organization keeps track of the stock. Inventory control applies to every item that is used in an organization to produce a product or service ranging from raw materials to finished goods. The process covers stock at every stage of the production process from the purchase to delivery to using and re-ordering the stock.

An efficient stock control system allows an organization to have the right quantity of stock in the right place at the right time. The process ensures that capital is not tied up unnecessarily and protects the production process if challenges are experienced in the supply chain.

Types of Stock/Inventory

The items that an organization uses to make products or provide services and run a business are part of stock or inventory. This inventory can be of four types;

i. Raw materials and components these are ready for use in production.
ii. Work in progress – stocks of unfinished goods in production.
iii. Finished goods that are ready for sale.
iv. Consumables – like stationery, fuel etc.

The type of stock or inventory can influence the quantity that an organization can keep.

Determination of Stock Holding Policy

The aspects that influence the stock holding policy of an organization will include;

i. The size and nature of an organization.
ii. The type of stock that has to be held.
iii. The space available for holding stock.
iv. The value of the stock.
v. The stock holding costs e.g. labor, security, equipment, storage, pilferage, obsolescence etc.
vi. Stock costs.
vii. Lead times.
viii. Price variations.

Stock Control Methods

An organization has to choose a stock control method or a combination of stock control methods that it can use to provide an efficient system for making a decision about what, when and how much stock or inventory has to be ordered.

Some of the stock control methods may include;

i. **Minimum Stock Level**

   An organization has to identify a minimum stock level and a re-order level, when the stock reaches that level an order has to be placed. This is known as the re-order level

ii. **Stock Review**
   An organization has to have regular reviews of stock. At every review that is done, an order is placed to ensure that stocks return to a pre-determined level

iii.   **Just-In-Time (JIT)**

This is a stock control system that aims at reducing costs by ensuring that stocks are at a minimum and stock items are delivered when they are needed and used immediately.

iv.   **Economic Order Quantity (EOQ)**

This is a system of calculating the quantity of stock to be ordered. Stock control software can be used to calculate the quantity to be ordered.

v.   **Batch Control**

This is a process where production of goods is done in batches. It is important for an organization to ensure that all the stocks/inventories needed are available for a complete batch.

vi.   **Fixed Quantity**

An organization may order its stock in fixed quantities. When another order is placed, the order may be placed at fixed intervals e.g. weekly or monthly. This can be a standing order which in essence has a control on the quantity and process.

vii.   **First In, First Out (FIFO)**

This is an efficient system that ensures that items that are in stock are issued or used in a controlled way to avoid deterioration of stock or inventory. It is useful for those who place orders to be aware of the use by dates of the materials.

viii. **Stocktaking**

This can be done on an annual or perpetual (continuous) basis to prepare a list of inventory, their location and value as a kind of audit to work out the value of stock as part of an accounting process.

ix. **Bar Codes**

These can be used to monitor and track the entry and exit of items into and out of an inventory system.

x. **Bin Cards**

This are stock cards that are maintained for each type of stock with information that describes a stock item, provides its value, location, re-order levels, quantities, lead times, supplier details and information about past stock.

xi. **Stock Book**

This kind of stock control system may be used in small stock/inventory systems where a book is used to indicate the stock received and issued.

xii. **Computerized Stock Control Systems**

This is a kind of integrated system in terms of invoicing, accounting, and pricing where the same set of data is used. It operates in such a way that the data is input once. The sales order processing and purchase order processing can be integrated in the system such that stock balances and statistics are automatically updated as orders are processed.

Inventory Ordering System and Economic Order Quantity (EOQ)

Depending on the needs of a given organization, an inventory ordering system has to be developed to ensure that inventory is obtained in an efficient and effective way. Organizations usually aspire to determine the optimal quantity that they need to purchase, that is, an Economic Order Quantity (EOQ) in order to maximize on the available resources while ensuring that inventory is available when required.

Inventory Ordering System

In an inventory ordering system, there are three types of data that are involved in an order – processing system. These three types of data are;

i.   Customer Information
ii.   Inventory Information
iii.   Orders Information

Customer Information

Customer information includes the name, address and a customer that identifies a customer in a unique way, this may be a code number or index number. In an ordering system or application this information is used in the actual order processing system. The customer data is accessed by those handling order processing. For purposes of entering orders, the customer information is available in a read – only access through a server or other means. Those who handle customer aspects and administrative aspects have access to customer information.

Inventory Information

Inventory information tracks the quantities of each item that is in stock or inventory in real time, that is, at any given time. The inventory data is available through a central server or other means available to the users. This information may not be accessible by those who handle order entry applications. This type of data is usually updated automatically and the figures kept current. In order processing situation data may be updated at given times and reports made available at agreed times that can be accessible through a server or other means.

In ordering systems that highly are highly integrated, the staff or those handling receiving of inventory or stock usually have access to inventory data; indicating the inventory depletion processes/patterns. This helps those ordering and receiving inventory to access crucial data for their areas of operations.

Orders Information

Orders information identifies items in inventory that a customer has placed an order for. The orders data set is a series of transactions. When an item is ordered it is usually recorded in an orders data set. It then follows that this order data is a time based record of events in the inventory control and management process. This enables the users to share this information through a server or other means. Orders data can be analyzed and appropriate decisions made regarding the inventory position.

Economic Order Quantity (EOQ)

The Economic Order Quantity (EOQ) is the order quantity that minimizes total inventory holding costs and ordering costs. The EOQ is one of the oldest classified production scheduling models. The objective of this model is to minimize the total annual costs. This framework or model is used to determine the order quantity. The framework or model is also referred to as Wilson EOQ model or Wilson Formula. The model was developed by Ford W. Harris in 1913, but R. H. Wilson a consultant who applied it extensively is given credit for the in-depth analysis that he gave the model.

The EOQ is applicable only when the demand for a product or item is constant over the year and each new order is delivered in full when inventory reaches zero. There is a fixed cost for each order placed, regardless of the number of units ordered. There is also a cost for each unit held in storage, commonly referred to as holding cost, at times; the holding cost is expressed as a percentage of the purchase cost of the item.

An organization has to determine the optimal number of units that it has to order so that it can minimize the total cost associated with the purchase delivery and storage of the product or item. The required parameters to the solution are, the total demand for the year, the purchase cost for each item, the fixed cost to place the order and the storage cost for each item per year. It should be noted that the number of times an order is placed will also affect the total cost, through this number can be determined by other parameters.

Underlying Assumptions of Economic Order Quantity

The underlying assumptions of economic order quantity are;

1. The ordering cost is constant.
2. The rate of demand is known, and spread evenly throughout the year.
3. The lead time is fixed.
4. The purchase price of the item is consistent that is, no discount is available.
5. The replenishment is made instantaneously that is, the whole batch is delivered at once.
6. Only one product is involved.

Inventory Costs

The main types of inventory costs can be described as follows;

1. Inventory Carrying, Holding and Possession Costs

These kind of costs include handling charges, the cost of storage facilities or warehouse rent, the cost of equipment to handle inventory, storage labor, operating costs, insurance premiums, breakage, pilferage, obsolescence, taxes and investment or opportunity costs. These are generally costs associated with not having inventory in an organization.

2. Inventory Ordering or Purchasing Costs

Inventory ordering or purchasing costs include the managerial, clerical, material, telephone, mailing, accounting, transportation, inspection and receiving costs associated with a purchase or production order. The other costs that can be categorized in this section are those associated with the identification of a supplier or vendor and placing an order with them

3. Set Up Costs

Set up costs refer to all the costs of setting up a production run. Set up costs may be substantial. They include such learning related factors as early spoilage and low production output until standard rates are archived, as well as the move, common considerations like setup employees' wages and other costs, machine down time, extra tool wear (depreciation), parts (and equipment) damage during setup etc. Both the purchaser's and vendors' set up costs are relevant. It should be noted that the reduction of setup costs and times allows for smaller production runs and hence smaller purchaser order quantities.

4. Stock Out Costs

Stocks out costs are costs of not having the required parts or materials at the time, when and where they are needed. Stick out costs include the costs include the cost of production output and lost sales both present and future, changeover costs that are brought about by the stock out, substitution of less suitable or more expensive parts or materials, rescheduling and expediting costs, labour and machine idle time etc. in most cases the consumer or user goodwill may be adversely affected and at times penalties have to be paid. In many organizations it is very difficult to assess stock out costs accurately. The general view is that stocks out costs are substantial and much larger than stock carrying costs.

5. Price Variation Costs

Often time supplies offer items in large quantities at price and transportation discounts. Where an organizations purchases small quantities – this may result in higher purchase and transportation costs. Where an organization buys in larger quantities – this may result in significantly higher inventory holding costs.

It should be noted that most of the inventory costs are difficult to identify, collect and measure. A buyer has to handle each case on its own merit when making a decision on inventory aspects.

Strategies to Avoid Project Delays Due to Supply Shortages

The strategies that may be adopted by an organization to avoid project delays due to supply shortages may include;

1. Those who are subcontracted on a project have to stick to the agreed work schedules.
2. Inventory that has a long lead time should be ordered in good time and time allowance taken care of to ensure that inventory is available when, it is needed.
3. Those who are charged with the responsibility of placing orders should provide accurate information so that they can get it right the first time.
4. Those who are in charge of a project should obtain appropriate instructions so that when a project commences it runs with minimum or no disruptions.
5. Effective determination of economic order quantities for the items that are needed for the execution of the project.
6. Work out an implementation and execution plan for a project in such a way that project tasks can proceed simultaneously e.g. when there is a shortage of given materials other tasks continue where the material in short supply is not needed.

Establishing Price

An organization has to establish or fix a price for its product or service that it presents to the market. Regardless of the type of product or service that is to be sold by an organization, the price that the customers are charged will have a direct effect on the success of the business. Pricing can be quite complex.

Basic Rules of Pricing

The basic rules of pricing are;

i.   All prices must cover costs and profits.
ii.   The most effective way to lower prices is to lower costs.
iii. Prices have to be reviewed frequently to assure that they reflect the dynamics of cost, market demand, and response to competition and profit objectives.
iv.   Prices must be established to assure sales.

Ways of Establishing Price

The establishment of price can be done through several ways that may include;

i.   Cost – Plus Pricing

Most manufacturers or service providers use cost – plus pricing. The main aspect to being successful with this method is ensuring that the "plus" figure not only covers all overhead costs but generates the percentage of profit that the manufacturer or producer requires as well. Where the overhead figure is not accurate, there is a risk of earning profits that are too low. The concept of calculating cost-plus can be seen in the illustration below.

Concept of Cost – Plus Pricing

Description	kshs
Cost of Materials	50,000.00
+ Cost of Labor	30,000.00
+ Overheads	40,000.00
= Total Cost	120,000.00
+ Desired Profit (20% on sales)	30,000.00
= Required Sale Price	150,000.00

ii.   Demand Price

Demand pricing is determined by the optimum combination of volume and profit. Products usually sold through different sources at different prices. This includes supply chains, retailers, wholesalers, direct sales, mail marketers, on line sales etc. The prices of goods that are sold through these channels are determined by demand. Usually a wholesaler buys greater quantities than a retailer. This makes the wholesaler to buy greater quantities than the retailer. This translates to lower unit price. The wholesalers' profits from a greater volume of sales of a product priced lower than that of the retailer.

The retailer typically pays more per unit because of buying smaller quantities as compared to the wholesaler and also sales less quantity. Due to this reason, the retailer usually charges higher prices to consumers. Demand pricing is challenging to comprehend because it is difficult to calculate correctly in advance the price that will generate the relation of profit to volume.

iii.   Competitive Pricing

Generally, competitive pricing is used when there is an established market price for a particular product or service e.g. where in market all the competitors are charging kshs. 1000 for a given service or product, then that is what should be charged.

Competitive pricing is mainly used within markets with commodities or products that are difficult to differentiate from each other. Where there is a major market player, commonly referred to as the market leader that will often times set the price that other smaller companies within that same market will be compelled to follow.

In order to use competitive pricing effectively, it is important to know the prices that each competitor has established. After this the organization can figure out an optimum price and make a decision, based on direct comparison, whether the price can be defended or justified. The organization establishing a price can decide to set a price higher than the competitors, the reasons for this could be the provision of superior service, warranty policy, after sales service etc. It is important that before a price is established, the organization acquaints itself with the level of price awareness within the market.

It is important to note that where competitive pricing is used to set the fees for a service, business, unlike a situation in which several organizations are selling essentially the same products, services vary widely from one firm to another. As a result of this a firm can charge a higher fee for a superior service and still be considered competitive within its market.

iv.   Mark-Up Pricing

Mark up pricing is used by manufacturers, wholesalers and retailers. A mark up is calculated by adding a set amount to the cost of a product, which results in the price charged to a customer. An example of this can be, if the cost of a product is kshs. 20,000 and the selling price is kshs. 24,000, then the mark up is kshs. 4,000. To calculate the percentage of mark up on cost, we can divide the percentage of mark up on cost $(4000/20000 \times 100 = 20\%)$.

This pricing method often times generates confusion and also lost profits especially among those who use it for the first time because mark up (expressed as a percentage of cost) is often confused with gross margin (expressed as a percentage of the selling price). It is important for those who use the mark up technique to fix or establish price to critically analyze overhead expenses (fixed or variable) and the cost of goods sold to effectively determine profit margin or gross profit margin in order to establish price for a product or service.

Review of Established Price

The price that is established for a given product or service need to be reviewed. The right time to review an established price may include;

i. When a new product is introduced into the market.
ii. When the costs change.
iii. When the service provider or producer decides to enter a new market.
iv. When the competitors change their prices.
v. When there is a change in the sales strategy.
vi. When the economy experiences either inflation or recession.
vii. When the customers are making more money due to the product or service [provided by the producer or service provider.

Quotations and Competitive Bidding

A quotation is a promise (which is usually submitted in response to a request for quotation) by a potential supplier to supply the goods or services required by a buyer at specified prices, and within a specified period. A quotation may contain terms of sale and payment and warranties. Acceptance of a quotation by the buyer constitutes an agreement binding on both parties.

Competitive Bidding

Competitive bidding is a transparent procurement method in which bids from competing contractors, suppliers or vendors are invited by openly advertising the scope, specifications and terms and conditions of the proposed contract as well as the criteria by which the bids will be evaluated. Competitive bidding aims at obtaining goods and services at the lowest prices by stimulating competition and by preventing favoritism. Competitive bidding can be done through open competitive bidding (open bidding) and closed competitive bidding (closed bidding).

Forward Buying

Forward buying is a practice that is used to purchase retail inventory in quantities that exceed the demand at a given time. In most cases this is normally done when manufacturers, producers or other suppliers offer temporary discounts. When the period for promotion expires, the retailer can sell the remaining inventory to consumers at regular prices. The retailer may earn huge profit margins. The retailers can sell their merchandise to the public at a discount that the authorized dealer is not allowed to offer. The discounts that wholesalers provide can assist in moving a large quantity of inventory from wholesalers or manufacturers especially when they need to reduce stock.

CHAPTER 4
PURCHASING MANAGEMENT

Objectives of Purchasing and Nature of Purchasing

The objectives of purchasing and the changing nature of purchasing include;

i.   Maintaining continuity of supply – the purchasing function has to ensure the continuous availability of materials, supplies and equipment in order to maintain production schedules and also to avoid disruptions in the production process or services delivery.

ii.   Maintenance of standards and quality – the purchasing function must ensure that materials and services that are procured have to conform to the required quality standards and specifications.

iii.   Avoidance of waste and obsolescence – the purchasing function has to order materials and service that are required and make proper decisions on the basis of accurate knowledge to avoid wastage and manage obsolescence of materials.

iv.   Maintenance of company's competitive position – the purchasing function has to help an entity to compete effectively in the market by purchasing the right and appropriate materials. The quality of an organizations output is to a great extent influenced by the quality of inputs like raw materials.

v.   Maintenance of the company's good image – the purchasing function has to create and develop a favorable image with the suppliers. This helps in creating cordial and mutual relations. The company can benefit from the favorable terms and that accrue from these cordial relations.

vi.   Developing alternative sources of supply – the purchasing function has to make deliberate efforts to crate and develop alternative sources of supply. This helps an organization to increase its bargaining base. In addition, the organization can be able to buy or purchase from alternative supplier if a given supplier is unable to supply.

Methods of Purchasing

The methods or ways through which purchasing may be done include;

i.   **Open tendering**

Open tendering is the preferred competitive public procurement method that is used for acquiring goods, services and infrastructure works. It is executed in accordance with established procedures set out in the procurement guidelines and detailed in standard bidding documents. Open tendering is also referred to as competitive bidding, open competition or open solicitation. The procurement notices that are used to call for bids for these requirements are known as invitation for bids or invitation to tender.

The basic or fundamental requirements of open tendering are that they should;

a) Be open to all qualified and interested bidders.

b) Be advertized locally and were required internationally.

c) Have objective qualification criteria.

d) Have neutral and objective evaluation criteria.

e) Be awarded to the least cost-effective provider.

f) Foster effective competition and add value for money.

Challenges of Open Tendering

Some of the challenges or disadvantages of open tendering include;

a) Lengthy time frame for completion of the procurement cycle.

b) This process requires strict adherence to procedures.

c) There may be lack of internal capacity for the completion of clear and precise specifications.

d) This process restricts suppliers, participation in determining the technical specifications.

e) Open tendering limits the possibility of an organization building long term relationship with suppliers given that different suppliers may be awarded to supply on different occasions that open tendering is done.

f) Open tendering only lays emphasis on least cost suppliers.

g) A lot of emphasis on procedures may limit the participation of a supplier in the open tendering process.

ii. Restricted tendering

Restricted tendering is a process where tenders or bids are only invited from suppliers, buyers, contractors or vendors who have been pre-qualified through a screening process. Restricted tendering is also referred to as restricted bidding.

A procuring entity may engage in procurement by means of restricted tendering when the nature of the goods, works or services that need to be procured are complex; where the time and cost required to examine and evaluate a large number of tenders would be disproportionate to the value of the goods, works or services to be procured; and there are only a few suppliers who are known in the market.

iii. Direct purchasing

Direct purchasing or direct procurement is a method of procurement that does not require the use of the competitive bidding process. Direct procurement is strictly regulated especially in public procurement process. An organization may use direct purchasing when the goods or services required are needed urgently and direct procurement is the most appropriate method. Direct procurement may be used if the value of what is being procured is low such that it may be uneconomical to use any other method of procurement.

iv. **Requesting Suppliers Proposals and Selecting Suppliers (Solicitation)**

A Request for Proposal (RFP) is the basic or primary document that is sent to suppliers that invites them to submit a proposal to provide goods or services. An RFP is designed to get suppliers to provide a creative solution to a business problem or issue.

Requests for Proposals are usually used when the project to be handled is complex and an organization requires the input of suppliers to suggest innovative ways of handling the project. In public procurement, Request for Proposal is specifically applied to consulting and other intellectual services such as design.

Benefits Requests for Proposals

a) Project stakeholders are be to visualize how the project will be handled.
b) Provides an opportunity for competitive bidding.
c) Helps the buyer to benefit from the innovations and creativity of suppliers.
d) Provides an opportunity to evaluate the suppliers.
e) Suppliers get an opportunity to submit organized proposals.

Challenges of Request for Proposals

a) The process consumes a lot of time.
b) Suppliers spend a lot of time and resources in the preparation of proposals.
c) Some suppliers may not respond to request for proposals.
d) It may be challenging to evaluate responses for Request For Proposals in an organization.
e) There may be lack of knowledge and expertise to evaluate responses to Request for Proposals in and organization.

Quality Based Principles

There are eight quality management principles that have been chosen because they can be used to improve performance and achieve success. These principles are;

i. Focus on your customer – organizations should understand their customer needs. They should meet and exceed the customer expectations.

ii. Provide leadership – leaders should establish unity of purpose and set the direction that the organization should take. The leaders should create an environment that encourages the organizations' objectives.

iii. Involve your people – organizations should encourage the involvement of all people at all levels and help people to develop and use their abilities.

iv. Use of a process approach – organizations can be more efficient and effective when they use a process approach to manage activities and related activities and related resources.

v. Take a systems approach – organizations should identify interrelated processes and treat them as a system. Organizations should use a system approach to manage their interrelated processes.

vi. Encourage continual improvement – organizations are more efficient and effective when they continually try to improve. Organizations should make a permanent commitment to continually improve their overall performance.

vii. Get the facts before you decide – organizations perform better when their decisions are based on facts. Organizations should base decisions on the analysis of factual information and data.

viii. Works with your suppliers – organizations depend on their suppliers to help them create value. Organizations should maintain a mutually beneficial relationship with their suppliers.

Purchasing for public utilities

The Public Procurement and Disposal Act 2005, the Public Procurement Regulations 2006, standard bidding documents, manuals and directions of the Public Procurement Oversight Authority (PPOA) provide the framework that give the institutional arrangements within which public sector utilities effect procurement and determine the subset of eligible members of the market (i.e. the private sector) for the procuring entity to do business with. In determining the eligible criteria, one needs to ensure that there is no prejudice whatsoever based upon any type of social discrimination.

A 'procuring entity' is defined by Section 3 of the Public Procurement and Disposal Act 2005 as a public entity making procurement to which the Act applies.

A 'Public Entity' is defined by the same section and includes;

i.   The government or any department of government.
ii.   The courts.
iii.   The commissions established under the constitution.
iv.   A local authority under the Local Government Act.
v.   A state corporation.
vi.   Central Bank of Kenya.
vii.   A cooperative society.
viii. A public School.
ix.   A Public University.
x.   A college or other educational institution maintained or assisted out of public funds or
xi.   Any entity prescribed as a public entity.

The public entities were classified by the PPOA in gazette notice no. 719 of January 2004, 2007 as follows;

Class 'A'

I.   State Corporation
II.   Ministries

Class 'B'

I.   City councils (Nairobi, Mombasa, Kisumu)
II.   Co-operative Society
III.   Universities

IV.   Colleges
V.   Judiciary
VI.   Commissions
VII. Parliament
VIII. District
IX.   Provincial Hospitals
X.   Semi-Autonomous Government Agencies

Class 'C'

i.   Other Local Authorities (Municipalities, County, Town Councils)
ii.   Schools
iii. District Hospitals, Sub-District Hospitals
iv.   Health Centers/Dispensaries
v.   Polytechnics
vi.   Constituency Development Fund Committees

The classification is not permanent and procuring entities are required to be on the lookout for any changes that may be made. Any procuring entity which is not sure of its classification is advised to consult the PPOA. Regulation 3 of the Public Procurement and Disposal Regulations 2006 in addition provides that "For the purpose of section 3 of the Act, Public Entity shall include;

i.   Anybody that uses public assets in any form or contractual undertaking including private partnership,
ii.   A company owned by the public entity to carry out functions that would have otherwise been performed by the public entity, and
iii. Any Body in which the government has a continuing interest.

Regulation 6(3) of the Public Procurement and Disposal Regulations 2006 provides that "the PPOA shall by notice in gazette, classify procuring entities either as Class A, Class B, or Class C, for the purposes of the 1st Schedule"

Responsibilities of the Accounting Officer/Head of the Procuring

Entity

The Accounting Officer of a Public Entity has the overall responsibility for the execution of the procurement process in the Public Entity, and specifically amongst other things shall be responsible for

a) Ensuring that the Heads of Procuring Entities within the purview of the public entity shall comply with the provisions under the Public Procurement and Disposal Act and the Regulations.

b) Ensure that the Procuring Entities establish tender committee in accordance with the Public Procurement and Disposal Act and the Regulations.

c) Ensuring that Procuring Entities establish a Procurement unit staffed to an appropriate level with procurement professionals.

d) Signing contract for the public procurement and disposal activities on behalf of the procuring entity for contracts entered into in accordance with the Act and the Regulations.

e) Ensuring that the procurement plans are approved and reviewed as necessary.

f) Any other functions provided for in the Public Procurements and Disposal Act, the Regulations or as may be directed by the PPOA.

The Accounting officer may delegate certain responsibilities to other staff in other staff in order to carry out the requirements of the Public, manuals and directions of the PPOA.

Responsibilities of the Head of Procuring Entity

The definition of a procuring entity has been given in paragraph 4.1 copy of the procurement manual. The person heading that procuring entity is the one referred to as the head of procuring entity of the purpose of the Act, the Regulations, the manual or any directions issued by the PPOA.

Further to the Section 3 of the Public Procurement and Disposal Act 2005 defines " Accounting Officer" as;

a. For a public entity other than a local authority, the person appointed by the permanent secretary to the Treasury as the accounting officer or, if there is no such person, the chief executive of the public entity.

b. For a local authority, the town clerk of the local authority.

It should be noted that some heads of procuring entities are also accounting officers when others are heads of procuring entities but are not accounting officers because they have not been appointed as such.

It is therefore clear that the responsibilities of the accounting officers and those of the heads of procuring entities are the same for the purpose of the Act, the Regulations, the Public Procurement and Disposal General Manual and any directions issued by the PPOA.

i. Establishing a tender committee in accordance with the procurement law and regulations.

ii. Establishing a procurement unit staffed to an appropriate level with procurement professionals.

iii. Appointing a procurement committee.

iv. Appointing an inspection can acceptance committee.

v. Signing contracts for the procurement and disposal activities on behalf of the procuring entity for contracts entered into in accordance with the Act and the Regulations.

vi. Ensuring that the procurement plans are prepared.

vii. Ensuring all contracts are complied with.

viii. Issuing as appropriate Administrative Guides to clarify and implement circulars issued by PPOA.

ix. Report to the PPOA in accordance with the directives of the PPOA.

x. Cooperate fully with any and all investigations carried out by the PPOA.

xi. Ensuring that all procurement procedures are properly documented and records and procurement and disposal files maintained in a secure location; and

xii. Any other functions provided for in the Public Procurement and Disposal Act, the Regulation or as may be directed by the PPOA.

Responsibilities of the Procurement Unit

In order to carry out and manage the procurement procedures each Procuring Entity shall establish a procurement unit and, where appropriate, subsidiary Procurement units. The size and level of stuffing of the Procurement Unit, and any subsidiary Procurement units shall be determined by the procurement and disposal workload of the procuring Entity, taking unto account the volume, value, complexity and type of procurement and disposal conducted.

The procurement unit must be staffed with procurement professional and may include staff with relevant technical skills where a Procuring Entity has a significant volume of specialized procurement or procurement requiring significant technical input.

The procurement unit shall be responsible for ensuring that any authorization specified in schedule 1 – The Procurement Thresholds Matrix of the Regulations and as specified in the Public Procurement and Disposal General Manual published by the PPOA and complied with.

Members of the Procurement Unit shall be appointed in accordance with the normal procedures applicable to the Procuring Entity, taking into account the certification and approval requirements which may be issued by the PPOA.

The head of the Procurement Unit shall be a procurement professional who shall report directly to the accounting officer or the head of the procuring entity.

Functions of Procuring Units

These are many functions and responsibilities that are to be carried out by the Procurement Unit. The main functions and responsibilities of procuring units include but are not limited to the following;

   a. Maintaining any standing lists of bidders or lists of pre-qualified bidders required by the Procuring Entity and liaise with the PPOA in aspects of the Authorities register of suppliers.

b. Prepare, publish and distribute invitations to pre-qualify, pre-qualification documents and invitations to express interest.

c. Receive, open and safeguard applications to pre-qualify and expressions of interest.

d. Evaluate applications to pre-qualify and assess expressions of interest.

e. Propose shortlists and lists of pre-qualified bidders to the Procurement Committee for approval.

f. Issue bidding documents to candidates.

g. Propose the membership of Evaluation Committee to the Accounting Officer for approval.

h. Co-ordinate the evaluation of bids.

i. Participate in or advise Evaluation Committee, as and where appropriate.

j. Recommend a negotiating team for appointment by the accounting officer where negotiations are allowed by the Act and the Regulations and participate in negotiations.

k. Prepare and publish notices of proposed award and notices of bid acceptance.

l. Prepare contract documents, in line with the award decision.

m. Prepare and issue rejection and debriefing letters.

n. Prepare contracts variations and modifications.

o. Ensure that procurement and disposal documents are issued and that records are maintained in accordance with the Regulations, maintain and archive documents and records of the procurement and disposal record for the required period.

p. Provide information, as required, for any petition or investigation to debar a bidder or contractor or any investigation under review procedure.

q. Manage all Public Public Procurement and Disposal Activities of procuring entity.

r. Implementation the decisions of the Tender and Disposal Committee including coordinating all activities of the tender committee.

s. Act as a secretariat to the tender and disposal committees.

t. Liaise with the PPOA Authority and other bodies on matters related to procurement and disposal.

u. Co-ordinate the advertising of procurement and disposal opportunities.

v. Prepare and submit to the Authority reports required under the Public Procurement and Disposal Act, the Regulations and guidelines of the Authority.

w. Monitor contract management by user departments to ensure implementation of contracts in accordance with the terms and conditions of the contracts.

x. Reports any significant departures from the terms and conditions of the contracts to the Accounting Officer.

y. Recommend for delegation of a procurement or disposal function to another entity by the accounting officer whenever a need arises.

z. Prepare consolidated procurement and disposal plans.

aa. Advise the procuring entities on aggregation and economies of scale buying.

bb. Co-ordinate internal monitoring and evaluation of the supply chain function.

cc. Carry out market survey prior to placing of orders or adjudication by the Tender committee.

dd. Conduct periodic and annual stocktaking.

ee. Certify the invoices and payment vouchers to suppliers

ff. Verify that available stock levels warrant initiating a procurement process.

gg. Carry out any other functions and duties as are provided under the Public Procurement and disposal Act and Regulations and any other functions that might be prescribed in circulars issued by the PPOA.

hh. In conducting its functions, the procurement unit shall at all times liaise with the following.

    i. The end user who initiated the procurement, to ensure that the procurement meets its needs.

    ii. The Procurement, Tender or Disposal Committee, to ensure that all required approvals are obtained promptly, and

iii.   The PPOA and other oversight bodies, to share appropriate information and facilitate the conduct of monitoring and other PPOA functions.

The Procurement Committee

Procurement Committees have the responsibility of ensuring that the selection of bidders are based on fair competition and in compliance with the legal and regulatory framework for the supply of goods, works and Services below the tender committee threshold. The opening of requests for qualifications by the procurement committee shall be done by the procurement unit and the user departments. The secretary to the procurement committee shall prepare the agenda for the procurement committee meetings.

Establishment of Procurement Committee

In each procuring entity, a procurement committee must be established to manage procurement requirements below the threshold set for the Tender committee in accordance with schedule 1 – The Procurement Thresholds Matrix of the Regulations. It is worth noting that typically this corresponds to the greater volume of the procurement procedures and so represents a considerable work responsibility.

The procurement committee shall be composed of the following;

i. An official delegated by the head of the procuring entity or the accounting officer who shall be the chairman of the committee.
ii. The finance officer or an officer carrying out related functions .
iii. Three other members appointed by the procuring entity or the accounting officer.
iv. A secretary who shall be an officer appointed by the head of the procurement unit.

The procurement committee may be permanent or ad hoc provided that the appointment of the members of the committee is provided by regulation 13 of the Public Procurement and Disposal regulations 2006.

All meetings of the Procurement Committee must be fully documented in recorded minutes which must be dated and signed by the chairman and the secretary after confirmation by all the members present. An original copy must be maintained in the procurement file.

If a member of the Procurement Committees is unable to attend a meeting, he or she should delegate his or her authority to an appropriate senior official who shall attend the meeting in his or her place, and consign his or her delegation in writing. The letter should be recorded in the minutes and attached. The chairman shall not delegate his/her authority to any other person.

It is the responsibility of the member who is delegating authority to ensure that it is to an official with appropriate at a meeting of the Procurement Committee.

Approvals by Procurement Committees

The Procurement Committee is responsible for reviewing the submission of the Procurement Unit for a particular procurement rejects the recommendation made by the Procurement Unit. In making its decision, the procurement committee shall state the reasons for its rejection or for clarifications and minor amendments. It must not request substantial modification to the procurement requirement and should not interfere with the award process. If a situation calls for substantial modification of the procurement requirement, then the procurement procedure must be cancelled and a new procedure initiated.

If the procurement committee has rejected a procurement requirement submitted by the procurement unit the procurement unit may resubmit the application with new information. The procurement committee cannot dismiss a submission on the basis of being a resubmission. Where any contract award or contract modification is beyond its authority level, the procurement committee shall verify the submission made and promptly submit to the tender committee, it should not attempt to deal with the case, recommend a course of action any other than submission to the tender committee, nor attempt to divide the submission to remain below the tender committee threshold.

Procurement Committee Meetings

The meetings should be attended by at least three members of the committee inclusive of the chairman, or their nominated representatives (quorum). Decisions shall be by consensus and where consensus cannot be achieved, the decision shall be through voting by simple majority and where there is a tie, the chairman shall have a second vote or casting vote.

The members, including the chairman, should declare immediately any conflict of interest or potential conflict of interest in any submission. In such a case, he or she should leave the meeting while the matter is considered and should not participate in the deliberations or decision making process of the committee in relation to that particular submission.

For technical and other matters, the procurement committee may summon independent advisers or members of the procurement unit to explain submissions or provide technical advice, where required.

The meeting of the Procurement Committee should be minuted by the secretary of the Procurement Committee, in particular the following matters should always be clearly detailed;

   i. A register of attendance,
   ii. The date
   iii. A list of all submissions considered
   iv. The decision made for each submission, including any major issues discussed, reasons for any rejections and clarifications or minor amendments to which the approval is subject.
   v. A note on the basis for any evaluation made
   vi. Any conflicts of interest declared by members and
   vii. Any dissenting opinions Procurement Committee members.

The quorum of a meeting of the procurement committee shall be the chairman and at least two other members. With the approval of the chairman a meeting of the procurement committee may be held chaired by a member appointed by the other members. The quorum must however be three including the chairman.

The procurement committee shall prepare quarterly reports of contracts awarded during the period which shall be presented to the tender committee and management for necessary action. The report shall contain at least the following information.

   i. Date of contract
  ii. Contract item
 iii. Contractors name
  iv. Total sum of all the contracts awarded during the period.

The procurement committee shall receive feedback from the procurement unit or the user departments where the contractors awarded contracts fail to perform for its directions or advise. The procurement committee shall refer any matters which are difficult to deal with to the appointing authority for necessary action.

The Tender Committee

In each Procuring Entity, a Tender Committee should be established. The composition of Tender Committees for different types of Procuring Entities is set out in schedule II of the regulation. Each member of the Tender Committee can delegate his/ her authority to an alternate who shall be appointed in accordance with schedule II of the Regulations, where any member is unable to attend a meeting of the Tender Committee the alternate has to attend.

The functions of the tender committee are given in regulation 10(2) of the Public Procurement and Disposal Regulations 2006.

The role of the Tender Committee is to perform the following functions:

   i. To review, verify and ascertain that all procurements have been undertaken in accordance with the Public Procurement and Disposal Act and Regulations, the Public Procurement and Disposal General Manual (PPDGM) and the terms set out in the bidding documents
  ii. To award procurement contracts where the value exceeds the threshold prescribed in schedule I – the Procurement Threshold Matrix.
 iii. To approve variations of contracts to previously awarded in accordance with the terms and conditions and the PPDGM

iv. To approve extension of the tender validity period in accordance with the regulations and the PPDGM

v. To ensure the availability of funds for the procurement under consideration.

vi. To ensure that the procuring Entity does not pay, excessive prices.

vii. Where aggregation has been proposed to review and approve the justification for such aggregation.

viii. Where lots have been proposed to review and approve the justification for the use of such lots

ix. To review the selection of procurement method and where a procurement method other than Open Tender has been used to review and approve the justification for the adoption if the procurement method in accordance with the Procurement Threshold Matrix.

x. To consider recommendations made by the Tender Evaluation Committee.

xi. To approve the amendment of contracts in accordance with the terms and conditions spelt out in the Regulations and the PPDGM.

xii. To undertake any other functions and duties as provided under the Act, the regulations, the PPDGM or instructions issued by the PPOA.

Approvals by Tender Committees

The tender Committee is responsible for reviewing the submission of the Procurement Unit and of the Tender Evaluation committee for a particular procurement requirement in accordance with the authority thresholds set in the Procurement Threshold Matrix. In making its decision, the Tender Committee shall state the reasons for rejection or for clarifications and minor amendments, it should not request substantial modification to the procurement requirement and should not interfere with the award process.

If the Tender Committee has rejected a procurement requirement submitted by the procurement unit or an evaluation report submitted by the Tender Evaluation Committee, the procurement unit may resubmit the application with new information. The Tender Committee cannot dismiss a submission on the basis of being a resubmission.

All decisions of a Tender Committee, including reasons for any rejection shall be recorded and modified to the Procurement Unit or the Tender Evaluation Committee in writing and in such a manner as to guide their work to re-submit their report or procurement requirement. It is clarified that the secretary of the tender committee is not a member of the tender committee and shall not participate in the deliberations or vote in the tender committee meetings.

Agenda of the Tender Committee

The secretary of the Tender Committee shall prepare the agenda for every item that will be adjudicated by the tender committee to case the work of the committee. The purpose of agenda is to ensure that the tender committee is given all necessary and accurate information for the purpose of adjudication and making informed decisions. The items of agenda shall have the following format:

  i. Title
  ii. Purchase item
  iii. Background information
  iv. Invitation of bids
  v. Submission openly of bids
  vi. Evaluation of bids
  vii. Secretariat comments
  viii. Request to the committee

The secretary must ensure that the agenda is brief, comprehensive, accurate and informative to facilitate speedy execution of the business of the tender committee.

Tender Committee Meetings

All Tender Committee meetings have to be attended by at least five members of the committee inclusive of the chairman, or their nominated alternatives, forming the quorum. The decisions of the Tender Committee should be reached by consensus or through voting by simple majority, or where there is a tie, the chairman shall have a second or casting vote.

The members, including the chairman, should declare immediately any conflict of interest or potential conflict of interest in any submission. In such a case, he or she should leave the meeting while the matter is considered and should not participate in the deliberations or decision-making process of the committee in relation to that particular submission rules on the tender committee are provided in regulations 10, 11 and 12.

The meeting should be minuted by the secretary of the Tender Committee; in particular the following matters should always be clearly detailed:

    i. A register of attendance
    ii. The date
    iii. A list of all submissions considered
    iv. The decision made for each submission, including any major issues discussed, the reasons for any rejections and any clarifications or minor amendments to which the approval is subject.
    v. A note on the basis for any evaluation made
    vi. Any dissenting opinions among Tenders Committee members.

The minutes of the Tender Committee shall take the form of the agenda but will have an added item of the decision of the Tender Committee. The decision of the Tender Committee must be very clearly recorded. Full particulars of the contract award must be recorded. The following information shall be provided;

    i.   Particulars of the procurement item.
    ii.   The contract sum.
    iii.   Full particulars of the contractor
    iv.   Duration of the contract or delivery period.
    v.   Other critical terms and conditions of the contract

Invitation of Observers and Advisers to Tender Committee Meetings

The Tender Committee may summon independent advisers or members of the Procurement Unit to explain submissions or provide technical advice, where required.

Regulation 12(8) provides that to enhance transparency of the procurement process the entity shall invite in addition to the representatives of various departments, at least two observers to attend its meetings in a case where the cost of the contract is estimated to be above fifty million shillings (kshs. 50,000,000).

Regulation 12(9) provides that at least one of the observers invited under paragraph (8) shall come from a duly recognized private sector organization or discipline relevant to the procurement under consideration. Regulation 12(10) provides that, the failure of an invited observer to attend a meeting shall not nullify the procurement proceedings.

The following are clarified in regard to the observers:

i.   The anticipated observers to be invited are to be decided on by the procuring entity and are expected to be stakeholders without vested or conflict of interest in the subject matter of procurement.

ii.   The observers may include representatives of such known professional or private sector organizations like Kenya National Chamber of Commerce and Industry, media, Kenya Association of Manufacturers (KAM) recognized Non Governmental Organizations (NGO's) organizations.

iii.   The observers invited are expected to attend as invited stakeholders who will be in attendance and will not participate in the deliberations of the Tender Committee.

iv.   As stakeholders the procuring entity shall not be expected to make any payments to the observers for their attendance unless the internal regulations of the procuring entity expressly provides for such payments or fees.

The observers may prepare reports indicating their observations made on the procurement proceedings conducted by the Tender Committee of the Procuring Entity. It should be noted that the observers have to be informed in good time before the date of the meeting to ensure they participate. Letters of invitation form part of the records to be kept in the file. The report of the observers will be kept on file but cannot be shared with any other organization, including the observer's organization. The divulgence of information that would jeopardize legitimate commercial interests or inhibit fair competition is considered an offence under Section 44(1)b of the Public

Procurement and Disposal Act 2005. The reports of the observer(s) where made should be copied to the Director General Procurement Oversight Authority (PPOA).

Tender Evaluation Committee

The main role of the Tender Evaluation Committee is to select bids based upon technical and financial considerations of the best submitted for a particular procurement request. It is important that the Tender Evaluation Committee has the appropriate competence to properly assess the bids and it is crucial that the highest ethical standards be applied in carrying out their duties.

Establishment and Composition of the Tender Evaluation Committee

Regulation 16(1) of the Public Procurement and Disposal Regulations 2006 provided that, for procurement with the threshold of the Tender Committee, the procuring entity shall establish an Evaluation Committee for the purpose of carrying out the technical and financial evaluation of the tenders or proposals. This has the meaning that for every contract award made by the Tender Committee there must be an evaluation report made by an Evaluation Committee. Every Procuring Entity and particularly every Tender Committee must understand this requirement. Regulation 16(2) provides that an Evaluation Committee established under paragraph (1) may comprise;

i. A separate Financial Evaluation Committee and a separate Technical Evaluation Committee, or
ii. A combined Financial and Technical Evaluation Committee.

It is therefore very critical for the Procuring Entity to decide how the Evaluation of the Procurement will be done and provide for it in the bidding documents. This is very important because the evaluation criteria to be applied to any procurement must be provided for in the bidding documents. Regulation 16(3) provides that an Evaluation Committee shall consist of a Chairman and at least two other members all appointed by the Accounting Officer or the Head of the Procuring Entity upon recommendation of the Procuring Unit.

Any member of staff can be appointed to be a member of an evaluation committee provided the person is capable of performing the work of the evaluation committee.

Regulation 16(4) provides that no person shall be appointed under paragraph (3) if such a person is a member of the tender committee of the procuring entity. It should be clear that an alternate member of the tender committee may be appointed to be a member of an evaluation committee subject to the alternate member not participating in the tender committee meeting in which the subject of procurement is adjudicated.

A member of an evaluation committee should have the following:

i. Knowledge of the overall operations of the procuring entity.
ii. Knowledge of the technical aspects of the procurement such as engineering, architecture, medical and pharmaceutical sciences, agriculture, information and communication technology and software development.
iii. Knowledge of the accounting and financial principles to secure financial accurate evaluation.

Functions of the Technical Evaluation Committee

The Technical Evaluation Committee is responsible for the technical evaluation of the bids received. The Technical Evaluation Committee has to ensure strict adherence to the compliance and evaluation criteria set out in the bidding documents. This is a critical function that requires technical skills, independence and understanding of the procurement requirement. No additional evaluation or compliance criteria outside of the criteria explicitly sated (i.e written in a specific section of the bidding documents to inform the bidders on the rating scheme and scale) in the bidding documents may be incorporated into the evaluation process. The technical evaluation committee must complete its report writing within thirty days after the opening of tenders.

The evaluation process is first and foremost a professional independent assessment of each bid and as such has to be performed by each evaluator independently prior to sharing his or her analysis, questions and evaluation including his or her rating with the other members of the Technical Evaluation Committee.

Three steps are necessary, these are

i. Reviewing, analyzing and making such diligence as deemed necessary for each bid to rate it accordingly to the grid established in the bidding document independently.
ii. Making a comparative analysis of all the bids received prior to finalizing his or her rating.
iii. Sharing his or her analysis and evaluation including his or her rating with the other members of the Technical Evaluation Committee.

The Technical Evaluation Committee shall then prepare a report on the analysis of the bids received, the ratings assigned by each member, the debate and discussion amongst members and the final ratings assigned to each bid(average of the final individual scores assigned by each member of the Evaluation Committee) and submit the report to the Tender Committee through the secretary. The reports must include clear recommendations to the Tender Committee to select the most qualified bidder or bidders pending financial evaluation. Where appropriate, the Technical Evaluation Committee may seek clarification on the bids from the bidders provided that such clarification is not for the purpose of introducing any new changes to the submission.

The members of a Tender Evaluation Committee should not enter direct communication with any of the bidders participating in a bid that such Tender Evaluation Committee is considering under any circumstances. In the event that a bidder has a constant with a member of the Tender Evaluation Committee, such contract and the circumstance surrounding such contract shall be reported in writing immediately to the appointing authority.

Functions of the Financial Evaluation Committee

The Financial Evaluation Committee shall be responsible for the financial evaluation of the bids received. It has to ensure strict adherence to the compliance and evaluation criteria set out in the bidding documents. No additional evaluation or compliance criteria outside of the criteria explicitly stated (i.e written clearly in a specific section of the bidding document to inform the bidders on the rating scheme and scale) in the bidders documents may be incorporated into the evaluation process. The evaluation has to be carried out within a period of five days from the date of completion of the technical evaluation. The financial evaluation committee shall use the technical evaluation report in carrying out its evaluation. It should be clarified that where the evaluation is by a separate technical evaluation committee and a separate financial evaluation report, the technical evaluation report shall be given to the financial evaluation committee directly without sending it to the tender committee. The tender committee shall be given the Technical evaluation report and the Financial Evaluation report at the same time together with the agenda prepared by the secretary to the tender committee.

It should also be clarified that where the Evaluation is by an Evaluation Committee which is mandated to carry out both technical evaluation and financial evaluation, the Evaluation Committee must complete its work within thirty five days from the date of opening of tenders. It is important to note that the evaluation of tenders may be complex and difficult. Apart from taking good care in appointing the members of the Evaluation Committee it is important that Evaluation Committees are appointed early enough to start the evaluation immediately after the opening of bids.

Each member of the Financial Evaluation Committee evaluates each bid independently. The financial evaluation is a two step process.

i.   Step 1: Review, analyze and make such diligence as deemed necessary for each bid to verify the accuracy, completeness and compliance to the bidding documents of the financial proposal.

ii.   Step 2: Share analysis, questions and evaluation including rating with the other members of the Financial Evaluation Committee.

The Financial Evaluation Committee shall then prepare a report on the analysis of the bids received, the ratings assigned by each member, the debate and discussions amongst members and the final recommendation of the contract award and the winning bid. According to the Public Procurement Regulations 2006, the Financial Evaluation Committee may seek clarifications from any bidder regarding the bid including correction of arithmetic errors provided that this will not lead to making any changes to the submitted bids.

The Inspection and Acceptance Committee

The Inspection and Acceptance Committee serves as an important element in ensuring that goods, works and services received are fully in accordance with the terms of the procurement contracts. This helps in enhancing the objective of achieving value for money.

Establishment of the Inspection and Acceptance Committee

Each procuring entity has to establish an Inspection and Acceptance Committee to enable the Inspection Committee to enable the inspection and where required to test goods received, or to inspect and review services, works and consulting and design in order to certify compliance with the terms and specifications of the contract and acceptance or rejection on behalf of the procuring entity the delivery of goods, works, services and consultancy services.

The composition of the Inspection and Acceptance Committee as per the Public Procurement and Disposal Regulations 2006 comprises a Chairman and at least two other members appointed by the Accounting Officer or the Head of the Procuring Entity on the recommendation of the Procuring Unit. The Inspection and Acceptance Committee may be permanent or ad hoc for the purpose of efficiency and practicality. The membership of the Inspection and Acceptance Committee is open to all members of staff with the relevant technical skills and subject to them being able to handle the responsibility of inspection and accepting or rejecting the procurement object. All three members should be present and sign the minutes and reports of the Committee meetings. Consultancy services may be excluded from inspection by the Inspection and Acceptance Committee where the Procuring Entity delegates inspection and acceptance to the contracting manager.

Functions of the Inspection and Acceptance Committee

After the delivery of goods, works or services, the inspection and acceptance Committee shall immediately;

i.   Inspect and where necessary test the goods received.
ii. Inspect and review the goods, works, or services in order to ensure compliance with the terms and specifications of the contract.
iii. Accept or reject on behalf of the procuring entity, the delivered goods, works or services.

According to the Public Procurement and Disposal Regulations 2006, the Inspection and Acceptance Committee shall ensure that;

i.   The correct quantity has been received.
ii. The goods, works or services meet the technical standards defined in the contract.
iii. The goods, works, or services have been delivered or completed on time, or that any delay has been noted.
iv. All required manuals or documentation have been received.
v.   Issue interim or completion certificates or goods received notes, as appropriate and in accordance with the contract.

Responsibility of the User Department

The end users are important elements in a procuring entity as structures that make up the procuring entity. According to the Public Procurement and Disposal Regulations 2006, the user departments are responsible for;

i.   Initiating procurement and disposal requirements and forwarding them to the Procurement Unit.
ii. Participate in the evaluation of tenders, proposals and quotations.
iii. Reporting any departure from the terms and conditions of the contract to the Procurement Unit.
iv. Forwarding details of any required variations to contracts to the procurement unit for consideration and action.
v.   Maintaining archiving records of contract management.

vi. Preparing any reports required for submission to the Procurement Unit, the Procurement Committee, the Tender Committee, the Head of Procurement Entity or the Accounting Officer.

vii. Undertaking conformity assessment of supplied goods, works and services with the specifications of the contract documents.

viii. Endorsing the issuance of goods, works and services received notes.

ix. Preparation of technical specifications and submitting the same to the Procurement Unit.

x. Assisting in the preparation of procurement and disposal plans.

xi. Making clarification on tenders, request for quotations and any other matter as may be required, and

xii. Carrying out any other functions and duties as may be provided under the Procurement and Disposal Act 2005, Public Procurement and Disposal Regulations 2006 or as maybe stipulated by the Public Procurement Oversight Authority.

Note: The user departments have to be involved actively in the procuring entity from the time of budgeting and preparation of procurement plans, to the inspection and acceptance of the procurement object.

Tender Opening Committee

The Tender Opening Committee is an important element in the procurement process. The Procurement and Disposal Act 2005 provides that, the accounting Officer shall appoint a Tender Opening Committee specifically for the procurement in accordance with the following requirements and such other requirements as may be prescribed.

a) The Committee shall have at least three members, and

b) At least one of the members shall not be directly involved in the processing or evaluation of tenders.

It should be noted that a person can be appointed to be a member of both the Technical Committee and the Tender Opening Committee.

CHAPTER 5

PROCUREMENT NEGOTIATION

Negotiation is any form of verbal communication in which the participants seek to exploit their relative competitive advantages and needs to achieve explicit or implicit objectives within the overall purpose of seeking to resolve problems which are barriers to agreement. A formal negotiation is an occasion where one or more representatives of two or more parties interact in an explicit attempt to reach a jointly acceptable position on one or more divisive issues about which they would like to agree. Each participant has implicit as well as explicit objectives which determine their negotiating strategies, for instance a supplier will explicitly wish to obtain the best price but implicitly will be seeking a contribution to fixed overheads and endeavoring to keep the plant and workforce employed.

Negotiation Styles

The negotiation styles or approaches that may be adopted in procurement may be classified as adversarial and partnership.

Adversarial negotiation is also referred to as distributive or win-lose negotiation. This is an approach in which the focus is on 'positions' which are staked out by the participants in which the assumption is that every time one party wins the other loses. As a result of this the other party is regarded as an adversary.

Partnership negotiation is also referred to as integrative or win-win negotiation. This is an approach in which the focus is on the merits of the issues identified by the participants on which the assumption is that through creative problem solving on or both parties can gain without the other having to lose. Given that the other party regarded as a partner rather than an adversary the participants may be more willing to share concerns ideas and expectations.

Characteristics of Adversarial and Partnership Negotiation Strategies

Adversarial Negotiation	Partnership Negotiation
Emphasis is on competing goals to be attained at the adversary's expense.	Emphasis is on ascertaining goals held in common with the other entity.
Strategy is based on secrecy, retention of information and low trust in perceived adversary.	Strategy is based on openness, sharing of information and high trust in the perceived partnership.
There is little concern for or empathy with the other party.	Each party is concerned for and has empathy with the other.
Strategies are unpredictable based on various negotiating 'ploys' designed to outmaneuver or 'throw' the other.	Strategies are predictable. While flexible, such strategies are aimed at reaching an agreement acceptable to the other party.
Parties use threats, bluffs and ultimatums.	Parties refrain from threats which are seen as counterproductive.
The approach is basically destructive.	The emphasis is on the use of imaginative, creative, logical ideas and approaches to a constructive resolution of differences.
The approach is basically hostile and aggressive, that is, 'us against them'	The approach is basically friendly and non-aggressive 'we are in this together'
The key attitude is that of 'we win, you lose'	Key attitude is how the respective goals of each party can be achieved.
If an impasse occurs the negotiation may be broken off.	If an impasse occurs this is regarded as a further problem to be solved possibly by intervention of higher management.

Conducting Procurement Negotiations with Potential Suppliers/Sellers

The process of negotiation falls into three distinct phases pre-negotiation, the actual negotiation and post-negotiation.

Pre-Negotiation Phase

This includes making preparations before the actual negotiation take place. The aspects or matters that need to be determined at pre-negotiation stage include;

i. Who is to negotiate – those to negotiate may decide to adopt an individual approach or team approach.

ii. The venue has to be decided on – normally the buyers expect the seller to come to them, in some instances the contrary may be the case.

iii. Gathering intelligence/information – this involves ascertaining the strengths and weaknesses of the respective negotiating positions, assembling relevant data which is to be presented at the negotiations, which may include relevant data on costs, production and sales.

iv. Determining objectives – the buyers should be clear as to what the negotiations are expected to achieve. Before the negotiations, the buyer should have a clear mandate from the superiors to settle at any point that does not exceed an agreed fallback position.

v. Tactics and strategy – a tactic is a position, maneuver or attitude to be taken or adopted at appropriate point in the negotiation process. A strategy comprises the overall tactics designed to achieve, as nearly as possible, the objectives of the negotiation. The tactics that should be decided on may include, the order in which the items will be negotiated, whether to speak first or allow the opponent to open negotiations, what time to make concessions, how to counter the opponents tactics etc.

The Actual Negotiations

The activities of the actual negotiation alternate between competition and cooperation. It is useful for a negotiator to recognize this pattern of interaction and to recognize the stage that has been reached in a particular negotiation.

Stages in the Actual Negotiation Process

Stage 1 – Introductions, agreement of an agenda and rules of procedure

Stage 2 – Ascertainment of the 'negotiating range' this may include the issues which the negotiation will attempt to resolve. With adversarial negotiations this may be a lengthy stage since the participants often overstate their opening positions. With partnership negotiations 'openness saves time.'

Stage 3 – Agreement of common goals which must be met if the negotiation is to reach a successful outcome. This will usually require some movement on both sides from the original negotiating range but the movement will be less or unnecessary in partnership negotiations.

Stage 4 – Identification of and, when possible removal of barriers that prevent the attainment of agreed common goals. At this stage there will be problem solving, consideration of solutions put forward by each party and discernment of what concessions can be made. During this stage, it may be useful to review what has been agreed, allow a recess for each side to reconsider its position and make proposals or concessions which may enable further progress to be made. If no progress can be made it may be decided to refer the issues back to higher management, change the negotiators or abandon the negotiations with the least damage to relationship.

Stage 5 – Agreement and closure, during this stage a statement setting out as clearly as possible the agreement(s) is drafted and circulated to all parties for comment and signature.

Post Negotiation

The post negotiation stage involves:

i.   Drafting a statement detailing as clearly as possible the agreement reached and circulating it to all parties for comment and signature.

ii.   Selling the agreement to the constituents of both parties that is, what has been agreed, why it is the best possible agreement, and what benefits will accrue.

iii.   Implementing the agreements for instance placing contracts, setting up joint implementation teams etc.

iv.   Establishing procedures for monitoring the implementation of the agreements and dealing with any problems that arise.

Ethical Vs Unethical Negotiations

Ethical Vs unethical negations may be seen in the table below

Ethical Negotiations	Unethical Negotiations
1. Negotiations provide reliable information 2. Negotiations done in good faith. 3. Participants honour their obligations. 4. Negotiators strive for win-win positions. 5. Negotiators avoid negative espionage 6. Negotiators conducted cordially.	1. Negotiators provide unreliable information 2. Negotiators not done in good faith. 3. Participants do not honour their obligations. 4. Negotiators strive for a win loose portion. 5. Negotiators may resort to negative espionage. 6. Negotiators are adversarial

CHAPTER 6

CONTRACT NANAGEMENT AND ADMINISTRATION

Definition and elements of contracts

A procurement contract is a written agreement between a procurement entity and a supplier, a contractor or consultant which is enforceable by law.

Contract management or administration is defined as the process of being responsible for the contractual obligations relating to managing an organization or a business in an entity.

In a procuring contract, the contractor has the responsibility of performing the contract as per the terms and conditions of the contract. The procuring entity has the responsibility of meeting its obligations of paying the contractors as per the terms and conditions of the contract. These are basic responsibilities of the parties in a procurement contract.

In order to ensure that both parties perform and meet their obligations, the procurement contracts must be managed. The procuring entity has to manage or administer the procurement contract to ensure that goods works and services are obtained as per the contract to achieve value for money

In the process of proposal development there are some terminologies which have to be defined these include;

Elements of Procurement Contracts

The elements of procurement contracts include:-

   i. The procurement file.
   ii. The contract file

iii. Contract administration Responsibilities.

iv. Procurement Contract Management Plan.

v. Maintenance of Risk Register.

vi. Measurement and Control of Performance.

vii. Control Review Reports.

viii. Payments to contractor.

ix. Contract Review.

The Procurement File

The procurement file is a crucial document in the management of a procurement contract the file is specifically opened for the purpose of processing the procurement before the contract is awarded. The procurement file contains the following

a. Procurement initiation requisition

b. All correspondence on the procurement

c. Bid document

d. Bids received.

e. Evaluation and award of the contract.

f. Information on the award of the contract and particulars of the contract.

The procurement file contains important information on the award of , and the particular of the contract hence it must be handled with caution.

The Contract File

The procurement and Disposal Act 2005, section 68(3) provides that no contract is formed between the person submitting the successful tender and the procuring entity until the written contract is entered into. The contract file shall be opened after the procurement contract is signed and it shall be opened by the contract manager. The file shall be used for recording the actual performance of the requirements indicated in the contract. The contract file should contain the following:

a. Signed original procurement contract

b. Any signed modifications to the contract.

c. Information on the performance.

d. Correspondence on the contract.
e. Contract correspondence between the parties.
f. Management progress reports.
g. Minutes of meetings of the project team
h. Payment records and close up documents.
i. Copy of performance security (where required).
j. Any other relevant information.

Contract of Administration Responsibilities

The Procuring Entity must designated a member of staff or a team of staff members as the contract Administration or responsible for administering the contract for each contract entered into. The Procuring Entity must issue a signed letter naming and appointing the contract Administrator that must be included in the procurement files and contract. The contract Administrator is responsible for:

i. Monitoring the performance of the contractor to ensure that all delivery or performance obligations are met.
ii. Ensuring that the contractor submits all required documentation as specified in the bidding documents, the contact and as required by law.
iii. Ensuring that the procuring Entity meets all its payment and other obligations on time and in accordance with the contract.
iv. Ensuring that there is adequate cost, quality and time control, where required.
v. Preparing any required contract variations or change orders and obtaining all required approvals before their issue such variations or change orders must be clearly justified in writing backed by supporting evidence.
vi. Managing any handover or acceptance procedures.
vii. Making recommendations for contract termination, where appropriate, obtaining all required approvals and managing the termination process.
viii. Ensuring that the contract is complete, prior to closing the contract file including all handover procedures, transfers of title if need be and that the final retention payment has been made.

ix. Ensuring that all contract administration records are complete, up to date, filed and archived as required.

x. Ensuring that the contractor and the procuring Entity act in accordance with the provisions of the contract.

xi. Discharge of performance guarantee where required.

Administration of sub-contracts

The prime contractor shall be responsible for administering any subcontracts and the procuring Entity shall monitor only the prime contractor's management of its subcontracts.

The procuring Entity shall not directly administer any subcontracts except where;

i. There is a risk of the Procuring Entity incurring cost or delay

ii. Successful completion of the prime contract is threatened.

iii. Special surveillance of high risk or critical subsystems is required.

Technical Inspection of Goods and Works

The Procuring Entity shall inspect goods or works at any reasonable time or place, including during manufacture or construction, prior to shipment, on delivery or completion, or prior to final acceptance, the procuring Entity may also inspect subcontractors.

The procuring Entity may observe tests conducted by contractor, or any subcontractors, under their own quality control procedures, conduct its own inspection, or employ an independent third party to undertake technical inspection.

Inspection and Acceptance of Goods, Works and Services

The procuring entity shall ensure that all goods, works and services are subject to inspection and verification by the inspection and Acceptance Committee, prior to acceptance.

The inspection and verification shall ensure that

i. The correct quantity has been received.

ii.   The goods, works or services meet the technical standards defined in the contract.

iii. The goods, works or services have been delivered or completed on time, or that any delay has been noted and appropriate actions as indicated in the contract have been taken.

iv.   All required deliverables have been submitted and

v.   All required manuals or documentation have been received.

The inspection and acceptance committee responsible for inspecting the goods, works or services shall issue interim or completion certificates or goods received notes, as appropriate and in accordance with the contract.

Procurement Contract Management Plan

The contract manager shall prepare a management plan which shall give a background of the contract and capture key focus area of the contract.

The procurement contract management plan shall contain the following;

a.   Background information
b.   Contract management team
c.   Contractor details
d.   Scope of contract management
e.   Key provisions of the contract
f.   Duties and responsibilities
g.   Communication channels
h.   Review and reporting requirements
i.   Activities and timescales
j.   Any other information which will assist the contract management team in its task.

Risk Management and Maintenance of Risks Register

Adequate measures/steps for risk mitigation must be taken in all public procurement contracts where the tender document so requires, unconditional performance security must be provided by the success tenderer issued by a reportable bank or a PPOA approved insurance company based in Kenya or by cash. Where the tender is international the security must be partly payable in Kenya shillings and be issued by local institutions.

The value of the two securities shall be in the same proportions of foreign and local currencies as requested in the form of foreign currency requirements. It should be noted that risk is the single word/aspect that determines the success or failure of every contract.

The failure of the successful tenderer to lodge the required performance security shall constitute a breach of contract and sufficient grounds for the annulment of the award and forfeiture of the tender security and any other remedy under the contract. In the circumstance the procuring entity may award the contract to the next ranked tenderer.

The greatest risks which might be mitigated in the management of procurement contracts are:

a. The supplier delivery late or not delivery at all.
b. The quality of the required goods, works or services being of inferior quality.
c. Being charged a higher cost than what the contract provided for.
d. The risk of paying for work not done.

A risks register should be maintained in which identified risks should be recorded and monitored.

The common contract risks that should be watched are ;

i. Incomplete or incorrect specifications.
ii. Poor communication.
iii. Suppliers lacking sufficient resources
iv. Production problems.
v. Quality problems including technology
vi. Shipment details.
vii. Underestimation of costs by supplier
viii. Inflation trends.
ix. Unexpected events.

It should be noted that any risks identified should be isolated and addressed before it is too late.

Measurement and Control of Performance

The requirements of the contract must be closely watched to ensure that there are no deviations or risks and those identified are dealt with in time.

Some of the aspects of measurement and control of performance include:

a. Cost overruns.
b. Effectiveness of communication
c. Input, process and outcomes.
d. Timelines.

Contract Review Reports

Where large procurement contracts are entered into, the management plan should provide for review meetings. Review meetings are held periodically as may be found necessary for the purpose of face to face communications of contract performance and discussing the way forward and preparing status reports.

After a review meeting a status report should be prepared to be shared by the parties which should include:

a. Execute summary
b. Report on performance of activities and budgets.
c. Other issues relevant to the contract such as environmental and general observation including the performance rating.

It is important to note that the contract manager has to report to the procuring entity's administration the outcome of such contract review meetings.

Payment of Contractors

Whereas it is important for the contractor to perform the contract satisfactorily, it is also important for the procuring entity to make payments to the contractor timely and according to the contract requirements.

Payments should not be made unless the invoice or the fee note is accurate and also submitted in accordance with the provisions of the contract.

Payments should be made to the contractor at the time they are done to avoid penalties and accrued interest and also a bad name or image. It is important for the procuring entities to plan their procurement and cast or fund flows to ensure that contractors are paid on a timely manner.

Contract Review

It is a good practice in large procurement contracts that after the contract is completed to contract close-out review. This should be done by the contract management team.

The review should consider the following

    a.   The timeliness of contract performance
    b.   Cost and quality performance
    c.   Risks analysis
    d.   Organizational and operational effectiveness
    e.   Appropriateness of the procedures
    f.   Suppliers performance

Once the review report is prepared it should be distributed as necessary. The report shall provide good lessons for the effective management of contracts to avoid failure of contracts. Where there is need the contractor has to be informed and appropriate taken for future contracts.

CHAPTER 7

GLOBAL SUPPLY

Global sourcing is the practice of obtaining goods or services from the global market or across geopolitical boundaries. Global sourcing often aims to exploit global efficiencies in the delivery of a product or service. These efficiencies include low cost skilled labor, low cost raw material and other economic factors like tax breaks and low trade tariffs.

Factors affecting international procurement

Common examples of globally sourced products or services include: labor-intensive manufactured products produced using low-cost Chinese labor, call centers staffed with low-cost English speaking workers in the Philippines and Pakistan and India, and IT work performed by low-cost programmers in India and Pakistan and Eastern Europe. While these examples are examples of low-cost country sourcing, global sourcing is not limited to low-cost countries.

Majority of companies today strive to harness the potential of global sourcing in reducing cost. Hence it is commonly found that global sourcing initiatives and programs form an integral part of the strategic sourcing plan and procurement strategy of many multinational companies.

Global sourcing is often associated with a centralized procurement strategy for a multinational, wherein a central buying organization seeks economies of scale through corporate-wide standardization and benchmarking. Global sourcing proactively integrates and coordinates common items and materials, processes, designs, technologies, and suppliers across worldwide purchasing, engineering, and operating locations.

The global sourcing of goods and services has advantages and disadvantages that can go beyond low cost. Some advantages of global sourcing, beyond low cost, include: learning how to do business in a potential market, tapping into skills or resources unavailable domestically, developing alternate supplier/vendor sources to stimulate competition, and increasing total supply capacity. Some key disadvantages of global sourcing can include: hidden costs associated with different cultures and time zones, exposure to financial and political risks in countries with (often) emerging economies, increased risk of the loss of intellectual property, and increased monitoring costs relative to domestic supply. For manufactured goods, some key disadvantages include long lead times, the risk of port shutdowns interrupting supply, and the difficulty of monitoring product quality.

The importance of global supply

One of the more surprising ways growth is being engendered in developing markets is by improving the way supply chains work. In fact, it's hard to overestimate the role supply chains play in laying the foundations of strong open economies. Effective supply chain management can have a positive impact on everything from the health of a region to its economic stability. The more people's wealth is subject to being part of a formal supply chain, the more they will recognize the need for an inclusive financial system — one being a by-product of the other.

Supply chains sit at the heart of economic development, this is the reason that is making increasingly making global producers to continue building relationships with the small, remote distributors of their product within a region. Proper supply chain visibility is always at the heart of these efforts.

Where as in previous years suppliers tended to lose sight of their products as they left the warehouse, by using modern technologies they can trace and monitor goods across their supply lines, manufacturers can reach out and advise customers on, for example, how best to store the products and deal with defects, etc.

The business case for supply chain visibility in developing regions such as sub Saharan Africa is all about enhancing the experience for seller and end user, and more so generating loyalty and transparency throughout the economic system. As sub-Saharan Africa's wealth grows, it could play a much bigger role in the global financial system, by connecting efficiently to the financial trading markets of the world via emerging technologies.

Selecting and managing off shore suppliers

Offshore outsourcing, a type of Business Process Outsourcing (BPO), is the exporting of IT-related work from the United States and other developed countries to areas of the world where there is both political stability and lower labor costs or tax savings. Outsourcing is an arrangement in which one company provides services for another company that could also be or usually have been provided in-house. Offshore simply means any country other than your own. The Internet and high-speed Internet connections make it possible for outsourcing to be carried out anywhere in the world, a business trend economists call globalization. In general, domestic companies interested in offshore outsourcing are not only trying to save money in order to be more price-competitive against each other, but also to enable them to compete with businesses in other countries.

Difficulties when buying overseas

The difficulties that may be encountered when buying overseas may include but are not limited to;
  i. Variations in material/service specifications and standards
  ii. Different currency for the buyer and supplier
  iii. Political regimes
  iv. Language barriers
  v. Time zones
  vi. Ethical aspects and expectations
  vii. Transport and logistics challenges
  viii. Long lead times

Payment terms, insurance and transportation

Incoterms

The Incoterms rules or International Commercial Terms are a series of pre-defined commercial terms published by the International Chamber of Commerce (ICC). They are widely used in International commercial transactions or procurement processes. A series of three-letter trade terms related to common contractual sales practices, the Incoterms rules are intended primarily to clearly communicate the tasks, costs, and risks associated with the transportation and delivery of goods.

The Incoterms rules are accepted by governments, legal authorities, and practitioners worldwide for the interpretation of most commonly used terms in international trade. They are intended to reduce or remove altogether uncertainties arising from different interpretation of the rules in different countries. As such they are regularly incorporated into sales contracts worldwide. First published in 1936, the Incoterms rules have been periodically updated, with the eighth version — Incoterms 2010 having been published on January 1, 2011. "Incoterms" is a registered trademark of the ICC.

Incoterms 2010

Incoterms 2010 is the eighth set of pre-defined international contract terms published by the International Chamber of Commerce, with the first set having been published in 1936. *Incoterms 2010* defines 11 rules, down from the 13 rules defined by *Incoterms 2000*. Four rules of the 2000 version ("Delivered at Frontier", DAF; "Delivered Ex Ship", DES; "Delivered Ex Quay", DEQ; "Delivered Duty Unpaid", DDU) are replaced by two new rules ("Delivered at Terminal", DAT; "Delivered at Place", DAP) in the 2010 rules.

In the prior version, the rules were divided into four categories, but the 11 pre-defined terms of *Incoterms 2010* are subdivided into two categories *based only on method of delivery*. The larger group of seven rules may be used regardless of the method of transport, with the smaller group of four being applicable only to sales that solely involve transportation by water where the condition of the goods can be verified at the point of loading on board ship. They are therefore not to be used for containerized freight, other combined transport methods, or for transport by road, air or rail.

Incoterms in Government Regulations

In some jurisdictions, the duty costs of the goods may be calculated against a specific Incoterm (for example in India, duty is calculated against the CIF value of the goods, and in South Africa the duty is calculated against the FOB value of the goods). Because of this it is common for contracts for exports to these countries to use these Incoterms, even when they are not suitable for the chosen mode of transport. If this is the case then great care must be exercised to ensure that the points at which costs and risks pass are clarified with the customer.

Rules for any mode of transport

EXW – Ex Works (named place of delivery)

The seller makes the goods available at their premises, or at another named place. This term places the maximum obligation on the buyer and minimum obligations on the seller. The Ex Works term is often used when making an initial quotation for the sale of goods without any costs included.

EXW means that a buyer incurs the risks for bringing the goods to their final destination. Either the seller does not load the goods on collecting vehicles and does not clear them for export, or if the seller does load the goods, he does so at buyer's risk and cost. If the parties agree that the seller should be responsible for the loading of the goods on departure and to bear the risk and all costs of such loading, this must be made clear by adding explicit wording to this effect in the contract of sale.

There is no obligation for the seller to make a contract of carriage, but there is also no obligation for the buyer to arrange one either - the buyer may sell the goods on to their own customer for collection from the original seller's warehouse. However in common practice the buyer arranges the collection of the freight from the designated location, and is responsible for clearing the goods through Customs. The buyer is also responsible for completing all the export documentation, although the seller does have an obligation to obtain information and documents at the buyer's request and cost.

These documentary requirements may result in two principal issues. Firstly, the stipulation for the buyer to complete the export declaration can be an issue in certain jurisdictions (not least the European Union) where the customs regulations require the declarant to be either an individual or corporation resident within the jurisdiction. If the buyer is based outside of the customs jurisdiction they will be unable to clear the goods for export, meaning that the goods may be declared in the name of the seller, in breach of the EXW term.

Secondly, most jurisdictions require companies to provide proof of export for tax purposes. In an EXW shipment, the buyer is under no obligation to provide such proof to the seller, or indeed to even export the goods. In a customs jurisdiction such as the European Union, this would leave the seller liable to a sales tax bill as if the goods were sold to a domestic customer. It is therefore of utmost importance that these matters are discussed with the buyer before the contract is agreed. It may well be that another Incoterm, such as FCA *seller's premises*, may be more suitable, since this puts the onus for declaring the goods for export onto the seller, which provides for more control over the export process.

FCA – Free Carrier (named place of delivery)

The seller delivers the goods, cleared for export, at a named place (possibly including the seller's own premises). The goods can be delivered to a carrier nominated by the buyer, or to another party nominated by the buyer.

In many respects this Incoterm has replaced FOB in modern usage, although the critical point at which the risk passes moves from loading aboard the vessel to the named place. It should also be noted that the chosen place of delivery has an impact on the obligations of loading and unloading the goods at that place.

If delivery occurs at the seller's premises, or at any other location that is under the seller's control, the seller is responsible for loading the goods on to the buyer's carrier. However, if delivery occurs at any other place, the seller is deemed to have delivered the goods once their transport has arrived at the named place; the buyer is responsible for both unloading the goods and loading them onto their own carrier.

CPT – Carriage Paid To (named place of destination)

CPT replaces the venerable C&F (cost and freight) and CFR terms for all shipping modes outside of non-containerised sea freight.

The seller pays for the carriage of the goods up to the named place of destination. However, the goods are considered to be delivered when the goods have been handed over to the first or main carrier, so that the risk transfers to buyer upon handing goods over to that carrier at the place of shipment in the country of Export.

The seller is responsible for origin costs including export clearance and freight costs for carriage to the named place of destination (either the final destination such as the buyer's facilities or a port of destination. This has to be agreed by seller and buyer, however).

If the buyer requires the seller to obtain insurance, the Incoterm CIP should be considered instead.

CIP – Carriage and Insurance Paid to (named place of destination)

This term is broadly similar to the above CPT term, with the exception that the seller is required to obtain insurance for the goods while in transit. CIP requires the seller to insure the goods for 110% of the contract value under at least the minimum cover of the Institute Cargo Clauses of the Institute of London Underwriters (which would be Institute Cargo Clauses (C)), or any similar set of clauses. The policy should be in the same currency as the contract, and should allow the buyer, the seller, and anyone else with an insurable interest in the goods to be able to make a claim.

CIP can be used for all modes of transport, whereas the Incoterm CIF should only be used for non-containerised sea freight.

DAT – Delivered At Terminal (named terminal at port or place of destination)

This Incoterm requires that the seller delivers the goods, unloaded, at the named terminal. The seller covers all the costs of transport (export fees, carriage, unloading from main carrier at destination port and destination port charges) and assumes all risk until arrival at the destination port or terminal.

The terminal can be a Port, Airport, or inland freight interchange, but must be a facility with the capability to receive the shipment.

All charges after unloading (for example, Import duty, taxes, customs and on-carriage) are to be borne by buyer. However, it is important to note that any delay or demurrage charges at the terminal will generally be for the seller's account.

DAP – Delivered At Place (named place of destination)

Incoterms 2010 defines DAP as 'Delivered at Place' - the seller delivers when the goods are placed at the disposal of the buyer on the arriving means of transport ready for unloading at the named place of destination. Under DAP terms, the risk passes from seller to buyer from the point of destination mentioned in the contract of delivery.

Once goods are ready for shipment, the necessary packing is carried out by the seller at his own cost, so that the goods reach their final destination safely. All necessary legal formalities in the exporting country are completed by the seller at his own cost and risk to clear the goods for export.

After arrival of the goods in the country of destination, the customs clearance in the importing country needs to be completed by the buyer at his own cost and risk, including all customs duties and taxes. However, as with DAT terms any delay or demurrage charges are to be borne by the seller.

Under DAP terms, all carriage expenses with any terminal expenses are paid by seller up to the agreed destination point. The necessary unloading cost at final destination has to be borne by seller under DAP terms. If unloading cannot be carried out by the seller, it might be better to ship under DAT (Delivered At Terminal) terms instead.

DDP – Delivered Duty Paid (named place of destination)

Seller is responsible for delivering the goods to the named place in the country of the buyer, and pays all costs in bringing the goods to the destination including import duties and taxes. The seller is not responsible for unloading. This term is often used in place of the non-Incoterm "Free In Store (FIS)". This term places the maximum obligations on the seller and minimum obligations on the buyer. No risk or responsibility is transferred to the buyer until delivery of the goods at the named place of destination.

The most important consideration for DDP terms is that the seller is responsible for clearing the goods through customs in the buyer's country, including both paying the duties and taxes, and obtaining the necessary authorisations and registrations from the authorities in that country. Unless the rules and regulations in the buyer's country are very well understood DDP terms can be a very big risk, both in terms of delays and in unforeseen extra costs, and should be used with caution.

Rules for sea and inland waterway transport

To determine if a location qualifies for these four rules, please refer to 'United Nations Code for Trade and Transport Locations (UN/LOCODE)'.

The four rules defined by Incoterms 2010 for international trade where transportation is entirely conducted by water are as per the below. It is important to note that these terms are generally not suitable for shipments in shipping containers; the point at which risk and responsibility for the goods passes is when the goods are loaded on board the ship, and if the goods are sealed into a shipping container it is impossible to verify the condition of the goods at this point.

Also of note is that the point at which risk passes under these terms has shifted from previous editions of Incoterms, where the risk passed at the ship's rail.

FAS – Free Alongside Ship (named port of shipment)

The seller delivers when the goods are placed alongside the buyer's vessel at the named port of shipment. This means that the buyer has to bear all costs and risks of loss of or damage to the goods from that moment. The FAS term requires the seller to clear the goods for export, which is a reversal from previous Incoterms versions that required the buyer to arrange for export clearance. However, if the parties wish the buyer to clear the goods for export, this should be made clear by adding explicit wording to this effect in the contract of sale. This term should be used only for non-containerised sea freight and inland waterway transport.

FOB – Free on Board (named port of shipment)

Under FOB terms the seller bears all costs and risks up to the point the goods are loaded on board the vessel. The seller must also arrange for export clearance. The buyer pays cost of marine freight transportation, bill of lading fees, insurance, unloading and transportation cost from the arrival port to destination. Since Incoterms 1980 introduced the FCA incoterm, FOB should only be used for non-containerised sea freight and inland waterway transport. However, FOB is still used for all modes of transport despite the contractual risks that this can introduce.

CFR – Cost and Freight (named port of destination)

The seller pays for the carriage of the goods up to the named port of destination. Risk transfers to buyer when the goods have been loaded on board the ship in the country of Export. The Shipper is responsible for origin costs including export clearance and freight costs for carriage to named port. The shipper is not responsible for delivery to the final destination from the port (generally the buyer's facilities), or for buying insurance. If the buyer does require the seller to obtain insurance, the Incoterm CIF should be considered. CFR should only be used for non-containerized seafreight and inland waterway transport; for all other modes of transport it should be replaced with CPT.

CIF – Cost, Insurance & Freight (named port of destination)

This term is broadly similar to the above CFR term, with the exception that the seller is required to obtain insurance for the goods while in transit to the named port of destination. CIF requires the seller to insure the goods for 110% of their value under at least the minimum cover of the Institute Cargo Clauses of the Institute of London Underwriters (which would be Institute Cargo Clauses (C)), or any similar set of clauses. The policy should be in the same currency as the contract. CIF can be used by any transport by sea and air not limited to containerized or non-containerized cargo and includes all charges up to the port/terminal of entrance. CIP covers additional charges at the port/terminal of entrance.

Previous terms from Incoterms 2000 *eliminated from* Incoterms 2010

While these terms do not feature in the current version of Incoterms it is possible that they may be seen in sales order contracts. Care must be taken to ensure that both parties agree on their obligations in this case.

DAF – Delivered at Frontier (named place of delivery)

This term can be used when the goods are transported by rail and road. The seller pays for transportation to the named place of delivery at the frontier. The buyer arranges for customs clearance and pays for transportation from the frontier to his factory. The passing of risk occurs at the frontier.

DES – Delivered Ex Ship

Where goods are delivered ex ship, the passing of risk does not occur until the ship has arrived at the named port of destination and the goods made available for unloading to the buyer. The seller pays the same freight and insurance costs as he would under a CIF arrangement. Unlike CFR and CIF terms, the seller has agreed to bear not just cost, but also Risk and Title up to the arrival of the vessel at the named port. Costs for unloading the goods and any duties, taxes, etc. are for the Buyer. A commonly used term in shipping bulk commodities, such as coal, grain, dry chemicals; and where the seller either owns or has chartered, their own vessel.

DEQ – Delivered Ex Quay (named port of delivery)

This is similar to DES, but the passing of risk does not occur until the goods have been unloaded at the port of discharge

DDU – Delivered Duty Unpaid (named place of destination)

This term means that the seller delivers the goods to the buyer to the named place of destination in the contract of sale. A transaction in international trade where the seller is responsible for making a safe delivery of goods to a named destination, paying all transportation expenses but not the duty. The seller bears the risks and costs associated with supplying the goods to the delivery location, where the buyer becomes responsible for paying the duty and other customs clearing expenses.

CHAPTER 8

LEGAL ISSUES AND ETHICS IN SUPPLY MANAGEMENT

Legal Authority of Buyer and Seller

In law, conveyancing is the transfer of legal title of property from one person to another, or the granting of an encumbrance such as a mortgage or a lien. A typical conveyancing transaction contains two major landmarks: the exchange of contracts (whereby equitable title passes) and completion (whereby legal title passes). Conveyancing occurs in three stages: before contract, before completion and after completion.

Procurement Laws

Public procurement law regulates the purchasing by public sector bodies and certain utility sector bodies of contracts for goods, works or services. The laws are designed to open up the public procurement market to competition, to prevent "buy national" policies and to promote the free movement of goods and services.

Dispute Resolution

Dispute resolution is the process of resolving disputes between parties.

Methods

Methods of dispute resolution include:

    i.   lawsuits (litigation)
    ii.   Arbitration
    iii.   Collaborative law
    iv.   Mediation
    v.   Conciliation
    vi.   Negotiation
    vii. Facilitation

Dispute resolution processes fall into two major types:

1. Adjudicative processes, such as litigation or arbitration, in which a judge, jury or arbitrator determines the outcome.
2. Consensual processes, such as collaborative law, mediation, conciliation, or negotiation, in which the parties attempt to reach agreement.

Not all disputes, even those in which skilled intervention occurs, end in resolution. Such intractable disputes form a special area in dispute resolution studies. Dispute resolution is an important requirement in International Trade: Negotiation, Mediation, Arbitration and Legal Action.

Judicial dispute resolution

The legal system provides resolutions for many different types of disputes. However, some disputants will not reach agreement through a collaborative processes. Some disputes need the coercive power of the state to enforce a resolution. Perhaps more importantly, many people want a professional advocate when they become involved in a dispute, particularly if the dispute involves perceived legal rights, legal wrongdoing, or threat of legal action against them.

The most common form of judicial dispute resolution is litigation. Litigation is initiated when one party files suit against another. In the United States, litigation is facilitated by the government within federal, state, and municipal courts. The proceedings are very formal and are governed by rules, such as rules of evidence and procedure, which are established by the legislature. Outcomes are decided by an impartial judge and/or jury, based on the factual questions of the case and the application law. The verdict of the court is binding, not advisory; however, both parties have the right to appeal the judgment to a higher court. Judicial dispute resolution is typically adversarial in nature, for example, involving antagonistic parties or opposing interests seeking an outcome most favorable to their position.

Retired judges or private lawyers often become arbitrators or mediators; however, trained and qualified non-legal dispute resolution specialists form a growing body within the field of ADR. In the United States, many states now have mediation or other ADR programs annexed to the courts, to facilitate settlement of lawsuits.

Extrajudicial dispute resolution

Some use the term 'dispute resolution' to refer only to Alternative Dispute Resolution (ADR), that is, extrajudicial processes such as arbitration, collaborative law, and mediation used to resolve conflict and potential conflict between and among individuals, business entities, governmental agencies, and (in the public international law context) states. ADR generally depends on agreement by the parties to use ADR processes, either before or after a dispute has arisen. ADR has experienced steadily increasing acceptance and utilization because of a perception of greater flexibility, costs below those of traditional litigation, and speedy resolution of disputes, among other perceived advantages. However, some have criticized these methods as taking away the right to seek redress of grievances in the courts, suggesting that extrajudicial dispute resolution may not offer the fairest way for parties not in an equal bargaining relationship, for example in a dispute between a consumer and a large corporation. In addition, in some circumstances, arbitration and other ADR processes may become as expensive as litigation or more so.

Online dispute resolution

Dispute resolution can also take place on-line or by using technology in certain cases. Online Dispute Resolution, a growing field of dispute resolution, uses new technologies to solve disputes. Online Dispute Resolution is also called "ODR". Online Dispute Resolution or ODR also involves the application of traditional dispute resolution methods to disputes which arise online.

Alternative dispute resolution

Alternative dispute resolution (ADR; known in some countries, such as Australia, as external dispute resolution) includes dispute resolution processes and techniques that act as a means for disagreeing parties to come to an agreement short of litigation. It is a collective term for the ways that parties can settle disputes, with (or without) the help of a third party.

Despite historic resistance to ADR by many popular parties and their advocates, ADR has gained widespread acceptance among both the general public and the legal profession in recent years. In fact, some courts now require some parties to resort to ADR of some type, usually mediation, before permitting the parties' cases to be tried (indeed the European Mediation Directive (2008) expressly contemplates so-called "compulsory" mediation; this means that attendance is compulsory, not that settlement must be reached through mediation). Additionally, parties to merger and acquisition transactions are increasingly turning to ADR to resolve post-acquisition disputes.

The rising popularity of ADR can be explained by the increasing caseload in many countries of traditional courts, the perception that ADR imposes fewer costs than litigation, a preference for confidentiality, and the desire of some parties to have greater control over the selection of the individual or individuals who will decide their dispute. Some of the senior judiciary in certain jurisdictions (of which England and Wales is one) are strongly in favour of this (ADR) use of mediation to settle disputes.

Salient features

Alternative Dispute Resolution (ADR) is generally classified into at least four types: negotiation, mediation, collaborative law, and arbitration. Sometimes a fifth type, conciliation, is included as well, but for present purposes it can be regarded as a form of mediation. ADR can be used alongside existing legal systems such as sharia courts within common law jurisdictions such as the UK.

ADR traditions vary somewhat by country and culture. There are significant common elements across ADR traditions. ADR is of two historic types. First, methods for resolving disputes outside of the official judicial mechanisms. Second, informal methods attached to or pendant to official judicial mechanisms. There are in addition free-standing and or independent methods, such as mediation programs and ombuds offices within organizations. The methods are similar, whether or not they are pendant, and generally use similar tool or skill sets, which are basically sub-sets of the skills of negotiation.

ADR includes informal tribunals, informal mediation processes, formal tribunals and formal mediation processes. The classic formal tribunal forms of ADR are arbitration (both binding and advisory or non-binding) and private judges (either sitting alone, on panels or over summary jury trials). The classic formal mediation process is referral for mediation before a court appointed mediator or mediation panel. Structured transformative mediation as used by the U.S. Postal Service is a formal process. Classic informal methods include social processes, referrals to non-formal authorities (such as a respected member of a trade or social group) and intercession. The major differences between formal and informal processes are (a) pendency to a court procedure and (b) the possession or lack of a formal structure for the application of the procedure.

"ADR" often refers to external conflict management options that are important, but used only occasionally. An organizational ombuds office typically offers many internal options that are used in hundreds of cases a year. These options include:

i.   delivering respect, for example, affirming the feelings of a visitor, while staying explicitly neutral on the facts of a case,

ii.   active listening, serving as a sounding board,

iii.   providing and explaining information, one-on-one, for example, about policies and rules, and about the context of a concern,

iv.   receiving vital information, one-on-one, for example, from those reporting unacceptable or illegal behavior,

v.   reframing issues,

vi.   helping to develop and evaluate new options for the issues at hand,

vii.   offering the option of referrals to other resources, to "key people" in the relevant department, and to managers and compliance offices,

viii.   helping people help themselves to use a direct approach, for example, helping people collect and analyze their own information, helping people to draft a letter about their issues, coaching and role-playing,

ix.   offering shuttle diplomacy, for example, helping employees and managers to think through proposals that may resolve a dispute, facilitating discussions,

x.   offering mediation inside the organization,

xi.   "looking into" a problem informally,

xii.   facilitating a generic approach to an individual problem, for example instigating or offering training on a given issue, finding ways to promulgate an existing policy,

xiii.   identifying and communicating throughout the organization about "new issues,"

xiv.   identifying and communicating about patterns of issues,

xv.   working for systems change, for example, suggesting new policies, or procedures,

xvi.   following up with a visitor, following up on a system change recommendation.

It is important to realize that conflict resolution is one major goal of all the ADR processes. If a process leads to resolution, it is a dispute resolution process.

The salient features of each type are as follows:

1. In negotiation, participation is voluntary and there is no third party who facilitates the resolution process or imposes a resolution. It should be noted that a third party like a chaplain or organizational ombudsperson or social worker or a skilled friend may be coaching one or both of the parties behind the scene, a process called "Helping People Help Themselves" – which includes a section on helping someone draft a letter to someone who is perceived to have wronged them.

2. In mediation, there is a third party, a mediator, who facilitates the resolution process (and may even suggest a resolution, typically known as a "mediator's proposal"), but does not impose a resolution on the parties. In some countries (for example, the United Kingdom), ADR is synonymous with what is generally referred to as mediation in other countries.

3. In collaborative law, each party has an attorney who facilitates the resolution process within specifically contracted terms. The parties reach agreement with support of the attorneys (who are trained in the process) and mutually-agreed experts. No one imposes a resolution on the parties. However, the process is a formalized process that is part of the litigation and court system. Rather than being an Alternative Resolution methodology it is a litigation variant that happens to rely on ADR like attitudes and processes.

4. In arbitration, participation is typically voluntary, and there is a third party who, as a private judge, imposes a resolution. Arbitrations often occur because parties to contracts agree that any future dispute concerning the agreement will be resolved by

arbitration. This is known as a 'Scott Avery Clause'. In recent years, the enforceability of arbitration clauses, particularly in the context of consumer agreements (e.g., credit card agreements), has drawn scrutiny from courts. Although parties may appeal arbitration outcomes to courts, such appeals face an exacting standard of review.

Beyond the basic types of alternative dispute resolutions there are other different forms of ADR:

1. Case evaluation: a non-binding process in which parties present the facts and the issues to a neutral case evaluator who advises the parties on the strengths and weaknesses of their respective positions, and assesses how the dispute is likely to be decided by a jury or other adjudicator.
2. Early neutral evaluation: a process that takes place soon after a case has been filed in court. The case is referred to an expert who is asked to provide a balanced and neutral evaluation of the dispute. The evaluation of the expert can assist the parties in assessing their case and may influence them towards a settlement.
3. Family group conference: a meeting between members of a family and members of their extended related group. At this meeting (or often a series of meetings) the family becomes involved in learning skills for interaction and in making a plan to stop the abuse or other ill-treatment between its members.
4. Neutral fact-finding: a process where a neutral third party, selected either by the disputing parties or by the court, investigates an issue and reports or testifies in court. The neutral fact-finding process is particularly useful for resolving complex scientific and factual disputes.
5. Ombuds: third party selected by an institution – for example a university, hospital, corporation or government agency – to deal with complaints by employees, clients or constituents. An organizational ombudsman works within the institution to look into complaints independently and impartially.

Benefits and suitability of ADR

ADR has several advantages over litigation:

i. Suitable for multi-party disputes
ii. Lower costs

iii. Likelihood and speed of settlements
iv. Flexibility of process
v. Parties' control of process
vi. Parties' choice of forum
vii. Practical solutions
viii. Wider range of issues can be considered
ix. Shared future interests may be protected
x. Confidentiality
xi. Risk management

However, ADR less suitable than litigation when there is:

i. A need for precedent
ii. A need for court orders
iii. A need for interim orders
iv. A need for evidential rules
v. A need for enforcement
vi. Power imbalance between parties
vii. Quasi-criminal allegations
viii. Complexity in the case

Ethics in Procurement

Some ethical concepts and principles that relate to the procurement process are:

i. loyalty and respect for rules and regulations.
ii. integrity.
iii. impartiality and fairness.
iv. transparency.
v. confidentiality.
vi. avoidance of appearance of impropriety.
vii. due diligence.

There are two definitions of ethics as follows:

i. The moral principles governing or influencing conduct.
ii. The branch of knowledge concerned with moral principles.

Ethics is the basis on which most of the procurement related principles, such as fairness, integrity, and transparency, are based.

Professional standards of ethical conduct, no matter what the organization, contain typical characteristics, including commitments to:

i.   Behave honorably in all aspects of work and professional activity.
ii.   Conduct oneself in such a manner as to maintain trust and confidence in the integrity of the acquisition process.
iii. Avoid "clever" practices intended to take undue advantage of others or the system.
iv.   Uphold the organization's standards and policies and all relevant legislation.
v.   Avoid conflicts of interest.

Codes of conduct

Organizations and professions often seek to address standards of conduct through the adoption of codes of conduct. Professional codes of conduct generally are written in broad conceptual terms rather than in specific situational or descriptive terms. They leave room for interpretation and often may seem ambiguous. Procurement professionals cannot abide merely by the letter of the law or the specific words in any code, but rather, they are guided by the spirit of the law or the broader concept that the code is intended to express. One reason why many procuring organizations avoid detailed and specific codes is these may give the impression that anything not prohibited is permitted or that anything not specifically addressed is not important. People in other professions who have not been trained in or are not appreciative of procurement ethics may not realize that a situation not specifically identified in the code may still be vitally important. Those who do not understand the foundation of a general requirement may not be able to apply a code in a specific situation.

No matter how hard policy-makers try, they will never specify in law, code, regulation, rule, or other written requirement everything that a procurement officer needs to know regarding what is allowed or appropriate and what is prohibited or shunned. It is necessary for procurement officers to understand what the law or rule is intended to accomplish.

Ethical risks and actions to manage them

Some of the common ethical risks in the procurement process include:

i. conflict of interest
ii. fraud
iii. corruption
iv. coercion
v. collusion.

Conflict of interest

A very common risk situation related to ethics in procurement is the risk of a conflict of interest. Conflict of interest can be defined as a direct or mutually exclusive clash between the interest of the organization and the private or personal interest of an employee engaged procurement in the organization.

In the context of procurement, members of staff charged with procurement responsibilities should:

i. Declare with immediate effect any potential conflict of interest.
ii. Not use information obtained for professional reasons for personal profit.
iii. Disclose and dispose the financial interest involved.
iv. Not participate in any conflicting procurement process.
v. Excuse or withdraw from any procurement process where the procurement officer may have a conflicting interest.

Declaration

It is good practice to have officials involved in the procurement process, including those participating in offer opening panels, evaluation committees or contracts committees sign, in advance of their duties, a declaration of no conflict of interest.

Honesty, truthfulness, impartiality, and incorruptibility are to be applied whenever a conflict of interest or the appearance of conflict of interest arises in the course of conducting procurement.

Gifts and gratuities

A common conflict of interest situation procurement staff have to face is whether or not to accept gifts from suppliers, partners or governments. Offering gifts to customers is a very common practice in the private sector. It is a marketing strategy based on the universal sense of reciprocity: if we receive something, we feel obliged to give something in exchange; i.e. there is no such thing like a "free lunch". Suppliers often offer different types of gifts, for example perishable products, hospitality, free training courses or experiences like exhibitions, fair trades, and sometimes in kind donations, etc.

Identifying covert gifts is not always easy, especially when at times, for example, training activities may be seen as beneficial for the organization; however, very careful review of the impact should be taken into account: would receiving the gift benefit one suppler over the others? Would acceptance be fair to the competitors? In cases where the content of such training / events is deemed appropriate and beneficial for the organization in a technical sense, self financial support, i.e. for travel expenses should be considered.

Fraud

Fraud means the intentional, false representation or concealment of a material fact for the purpose of inducing another to act upon it to his/her detriment, for example in order to influence the competitive selection process or the execution of a contract.

There are four common fraud scenarios in procurement. These are:

i.   A person with responsibility for buying defrauds his or her employer.
ii. Suppliers defraud their customers.
iii. Suppliers and buyers work together to defraud the buyer's employer.
iv. Buyers make personal gain at the expense of the supplier.

Corruption

Corruption means the practice of offering, giving, receiving, or soliciting, directly or indirectly anything of value to influence the action of a public official in the competitive selection process or in contract execution.

There are two common types of corruption:

Direct approach which includes;

i. Cash paid to the procurement officer, to settle the buyer's personal debts or paid to a third party for the buyer's benefit.
ii. Cheques paid directly to the buyer or members of his family, paid to businesses in which the buyer has an interest.
iii. Cheques paid to settle the buyer's personal debts.
iv. Shares and share options.
v. Free or discounted goods or services.

Indirect approach which includes;

i. Employment of a member of the buyer's family, or employment of the buyer on a consultancy basis.
ii. Future offers of the same.
iii. Inside information which will benefit the buyer.
iv. Threats of blackmail or violence.
v. Free travel and expenses to visit exhibitions or to visit suppliers' factories.
vi. Invitation to entertainment events.

Coercion

Coercion means harming or threatening to harm, directly or indirectly, persons, or their property to influence their participation in the procurement process, or affect the execution of a contract.

Collusion

Collusion means a scheme or an arrangement between two or more suppliers, with or without knowledge of the buying organization, designed to establish prices at artificial, non-competitive levels.

Potential areas of risk in the procurement cycle

Some potential areas of risk relating to ethics in the procurement cycle may include;

i. Budgeting - Fraud and corruption must be paid for from somewhere. Lack of proper budgetary control, for example when all funds are not allocated to a specific purpose, can provide the necessary funds.

ii. Financial approval policy - Without regular audits and strict management controls, there are opportunities for fraudulent use of a person's own levels of authority, or of misusing someone else's.

iii. Perceived need - Requirements can be invented or falsified.

iv. Specification development - Specifications can be written to favor a specific supplier. Clarifications on specifications can be provided to one of the invitees only during the tendering process.

v. Evaluation criteria - Evaluation criteria can be written, or amended, after receipt of offers to favor a particular supplier.

vi. Pre-qualification - This process can be used to limit the field of competition to give a favored supplier an advantage.

vii. Invitation to tender/sourcing - This process can be used to give the illusion of competition where it does not really exists by inviting tenders from companies who are known to be unsatisfactory, or by not sending out complete specifications to all tenders at the same time etc.

viii. Offer evaluation - Fraud at this stage occurs mainly when objective evaluation criteria have not been agreed in advance. It can also occur where technical staff is able to use their specialist knowledge to mislead other members of the evaluation team.

ix. Negotiation - Favoured suppliers can be assisted or given useful information during negotiations.

x. Contract award - There are opportunities for fraud by the supplier either through deliberately fraudulent acts or through buyer incompetence.

xi. Post award changes to specifications - This allows suppliers to increase profits, particularly when awarded the contract on an attractively low offer price.

xii. Goods receipt - Examples are: Allowing under-deliveries of goods or non-performance to specifications, or drafting false goods inward notes; deliberate over ordering; allowing inventory to dwindle so that emergency orders at a higher price will have to be processed.

xiii. Invoice certification - Deliberate overcharging, backdating orders to allow benefit from price changes, paying twice, failing to insist on or monitor retentions.

xiv. Decentralized procurement organization - In decentralized organizations the responsibilities are delegated to a large number of people, and it is difficult for the central procurement function to exercise total control and to be aware of what is going on in the decentralized units. Although decentralization can often improve efficiency and reduce costs, it can also increase the risks of corruption.

Potential warning signs of unethical practices

There are some typical signs that may indicate or warn of unethical practices. These include, but are not limited to the following:

i. deviations from correct procedures
ii. overcharging by the supplier
iii. poor record keeping
iv. missing files
v. poor or no separation of duties (for example, the same person issues the order and approves the payment)
vi. poor control (for example, only one person signs a contract)
vii. buyer's extravagant life style
viii. buyer's frequent absence from the office
ix. excessive entertaining by suppliers
x. resistance to audit
xi. reluctance to delegate
xii. excessive secrecy
xiii. dictatorial management style
xiv. unnecessary meetings with suppliers
xv. not allowing other staff to deal with certain suppliers
xvi. established suppliers' reluctance of entering competitive tendering
xvii. supplier cartels.

Tools and mechanisms to prevent and detect unethical practices

Some tools and mechanisms that may be used to prevent and detect the occurrence of unethical practices are listed below.

Management responsibility

Management should maintain the highest standards of integrity in its everyday dealings. Where senior management behaves dishonestly, corruption and fraud will spread to all levels.

Management's responsibility is to set the highest standards of integrity and be an example for everybody in the organization to follow. Managers should also point out correct behavior to employees and draw the line between acceptable and unacceptable behavior.

Management is also ultimately responsible for the operations and assets under their command. It is their responsibility and in their interest to ensure that the organization has the necessary procedures and control systems in place to ensure maximum security and minimize the risk of corruption and fraud.

Code of ethics

All organizations should develop a code of ethics for all staff to follow. A code of ethics is a formalized statement containing ethical codes of conduct for the organizations' members to follow. The Code of Ethics will clearly state what type of behavior is expected from the members, and what type of behavior is unacceptable.

Organizational procedures

To prevent fraud and corruption an organization should formulate and follow organizational procedures that may include:

i.   Pre-employment screening - The background of all job applicants should be checked before they are employed and granted access to premises and assets.
ii. Classification and protection of information - 'Clear desk policy', secure filing cabinets for all employees, sufficient number of paper shredders, secure disposal of all waste paper
iii. Data security standards - Procedures should be introduced for all data processing resources. Instructions on minimum standards should be enforced
iv. Incident reporting - All employees should be responsible for reporting losses and security incidents; and all incidents, regardless of how small they are, should be reported.

Human resource policies and procedures

Fair, open, and efficient human resource policies and procedures reduce the organization's exposure to fraud. Organizations should consider the following factors in their human resource policies and procedures;

i.   Job descriptions - Security responsibilities should be drafted into contracts and job descriptions to deter personnel from being dishonest.

ii.   Education and training - Awareness training can clarify what is meant by ethical conduct, short cuts, and fraud and contribute to the prevention of fraud; Training programs can be supported by booklets on the organization's business ethics and security policies, articles in internal newsletters or magazines, newsletters including reports on frauds discovered and the lessons learned from them, as well as films and videos; and New employee induction training can cover security.

iii.   Investigation - Set down organizational rules for conducting investigations into suspected or reported incidents of fraud or breaches of security, including employee obligations to assist in such investigations; and Criminal offences or reasons for disciplinary action should be brought to the attention of all staff.

Accounting controls

The integrity of accounting systems is an essential element in preventing fraud. Controls should ensure that details of all goods and equipment moving in and out of the organization are recorded on serially numbered documents or computer records, and copies of documents recording movements are retained securely. Maximum use should be made of numerical controls, using documents with pre-printed serial numbers.

Levels of authority to approve accounting transactions should be clearly defined and regularly audited. Each system should define who will be held responsible for losses, errors and concealment. Areas of responsibility should be identified and enforced. Books and records should be protected in the same way as all of the assets of the organization.

Segregation of duties

This is the most basic and one of the most effective ways of preventing fraud, since it removes the possibility of 'closed loops', that is, one person having the authority to budget, provision, order and pay. Each transaction should be divided into a number of stages and no one person should ever have the authority to handle all of the stages.

Control systems

Control systems in procurement protect honest buyers and suppliers from false accusations of dishonesty, encourage them to work honestly and effectively, and prevent and detect corruption.

It is often difficult to get the right balance between under- and over-control and many organizations have control systems which are either too restrictive or too lax. An effective and well-balanced control system needs to be flexible, allowing honest buyers and suppliers to operate efficiently, while at the same time minimizing the risks of dishonesty.

Controls in procurement

Procurement procedures should be set out in a manual provided to all staff involved in procurement. Procedures, authorities, responsibilities and penalties for not adhering to procedures should be clearly defined. When setting the strategy for a particular procurement, the following factors should be taken into account:

i. The threshold above which contracts and orders must be put out for competitive tenders should be clearly defined and enforced.
ii. As far as possible, spot, short-term, or emergency orders should be avoided.
iii. Cost-plus contracts should be avoided if possible, but if they cannot be avoided special care should be taken to verify the supplier's expenses.

Financial approval policy

The policy on financial approval for procurement actions should be clearly communicated to all relevant staff. The consequence of abuse should be defined. Approval levels should not be set artificially low, but at a realistic level sufficient to enable employees to do their jobs efficiently.

Standard terms and conditions of contract, and standard forms should be included in all solicitation documents as well as in all contracts and purchase orders. Standard forms used in procurement should be developed.

CHAPTER 9

SUPPLY PROCESS AND TECHNOLOGY

Information Systems and the Supply Process

Today Information systems have matured and are there to stay. Your competitiveness in business highly depends on how effective your information system is, in keeping you at the edge. Competitors are always on the lookout and shopping for the latest software that can help them stay at the edge, maintain a healthy supply chain cost effectively and ameliorate their profit margins. Customers on the other hand are look for a supplier who will supply quality goods promptly at the cheapest price. The only choice that supply chain managers have is to use information systems that will help them cut on cost and supply goods promptly within and without their target markets promptly. Such information systems also enable them to track goods while in transit, update the customer on the status of the shipment on transit and reduce pilferage.

When seeking to use an information system in the supply process, there is need to look at the supply process holistically. It should be noted that information systems must be appropriately mapped to the right supply process in order for an organization to fully benefit from the information system. In addition to that, it should also be noted that only appropriate areas in the supply process need to be mapped with information system to avoid wastage in terms implementation of information systems that do not add value to the supply process. When mapping the information systems to the supply process, you should consider:

1. Supply, product , demand and income
2. The process disciplines that fall under the supply i.e. the strategic network, procurement, production, sourcing and planning.
3. The process disciplines that fall under the product i.e. product design and production
4. The process disciplines that fall under the demand management i.e. customer relations management(CRM) and demand fulfillment
5. The process disciplines that fall under income i.e. cash management
6. Organization functions i.e. the shared resources across the organization like legal, administration, finance , human resource etc
7. Information technology which cut across the entire organization and finally the
8. Executive leadership which also cut across the entire organization

Technology Drivers System

Information Technology is a major contributor in Supply Chain Management (SCM) today. It is applied in the following areas in SCM:

1. Supply chain planning and collaboration with a view of sharing planning, inventory and production information
2. Transaction processing to accelerate efficiency of repetitive information exchanges between supply chain partners.
3. Order tracking and delivery coordination for timely delivery of goods and services

The major drivers of technology in SCM are:

1. Need for a software solution that would allow more flexibility in identify market trends faster in order to take advantage of.
2. Now that the world has become a global village, there is need for supply chain firm to have end-to-end shipment visibility around the world.
3. There is greater need for demand planning system
4. Unpredictable and logically demanding competitive business environments
5. Need for better planning and timely communication within the business environment
6. Cost reduction
7. High volume of business transactions
8. Need for real time monitoring of good while on transit
9. Need for reduction of paper work in supply chain management systems and procurement systems.

E-commerce and E-procurement and E-Supply Chain Management

E-Commerce

Many businesses are taking advantage of E-commerce as a way in which the can get to customers all over the world without being restricted with working hours , local legislation or who to conduct business with. The speed of e-commerce has affected the structure of market all over the world by allowing firms to bypass intermediaries in the supply chain and deal directly with the customers. In Kenya systems like OLX have redefined the market structure by allowing any one to supply and buy anything anytime without considering market structures hence making costs of goods to go down. The high speed connectivity of e-commerce also contributes to new market structures through the access it provides to new customers all over the world. New business have also emerged and taken advantage of high speed internet and convenience. In Kenya in the past if you need banking services, you could only be supplied by banks. Today mobile money transfer system has affected this supply chain. A good example is Mpesa, Nation Hela etc. This has forced the banking sector to change how the how they conduct business buy integrating mobile banking systems to their banking systems. An example is mobile withdrawal and deposit system offered by Kenya Commercial Bank.

E-Procurement

E-Procurement are being used today to ensure that goods and services are at the right price, delivered at the right time, are of the right quality, of the right quantity, and are from the right source. The advantages of e-procurement systems are:

i. Enhanced budgetary control
ii. The reduce of administrative errors and costs
iii. Standardization and consolidation of buys hence making it easy for there needs to be met.
iv. Improve information management by making information easily available whenever needed
v. Improve payment process since it can be integrated with other e-payment systems
vi. Reduced purchasing cycle time and cost

An example of e-procurement system is one that is being implemented by Kenyan National Treasury under the Financial Management Information System (IFMIS)

E-Supply Chain Management

The trends in e-commerce have not left behind the supply chain industry.

E-Supply Chain Management (E-SCM) systems have emanated. E-SCM has the following advantages:

i. It reduces complexities of supply chain intermediaries
ii. It is more efficient, more efficient and cost effective as compared to traditional supply chain management information systems
iii. Has better data integration
iv. Can be managed from anywhere around the world.

Examples of E-SCM available are web based order tracking, web based shipment tracking, electronic data interchange of invoice and payment etc

Bar-coding

A barcodes is a machine-readable code composed of a pattern of parallel lines of varying widths and a number that are printed for purposes of identifying product. They play a big role in inventory management. They make business integration processes in logistic and supply chain management efficient. They help track product and reduce error. They are acceptable worldwide in logistic and supply chain management because they are:

i. Affordable
ii. Accurate
iii. Help in identification of fast-selling and slow-selling items so that they can be reordered or not ordered
iv. The technology enables timely and accurate information that helps to operate with greater warehouse efficiency.
v. Help in keeping product historical data accurately
vi. Help track products from one distribution centre to another

There are two types of barcode namely linear and matrix barcode.

Linear barcodes are first generation barcode and are one dimensional in nature. They are made up of lines and spaces of various widths that create specific patterns of information that can be scanned using a barcode reader. Matrix barcode represents information in two-dimensional way hence represents more data per unit than a linear barcode. To read the information encoded in the barcode, a barcode scanner must be used.

Figure 1: Linear barcodes

Figure 2: Matrix (2D) barcodes

Figure 2: Matrix barcode

Electronic Data Interchange (EDI)

Electronic Data Interchange (EDI) is an electronic communication system that provides standards for exchanging business data. It is also computer-to-computer exchange of business documents in a standard electronic format between business partners. There is no paperwork involved in electronic data interchange hence money that could have been used in producing different business documents is saved. EDI is faster than the conventional methods of conducting business because the system is fast.

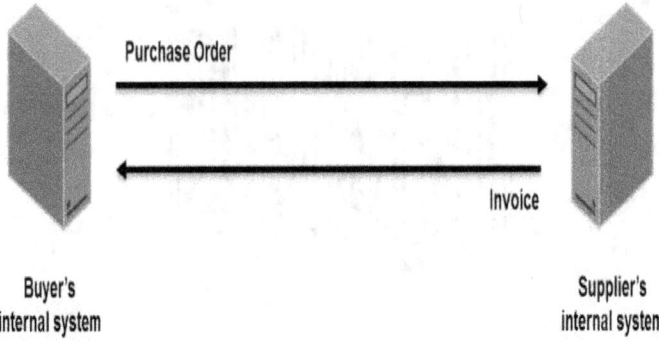

i. In EDI Buyer makes a buying decision, creates the purchase order but does not print it,

ii. EDI software creates an electronic version of the purchase order and transmits it automatically to the supplier.

iii. Supplier's order entry system receives the purchase order and updates the system immediately on receipt.

Supplier's order entry system creates an acknowledgment and transmits it back to confirm receipt.

References

Government of Kenya, The Public Procurement and Disposal Act 2005,

Government of Kenya, The Public Procurement Regulations 2006,

International Chamber of Commerce, Incoterms 2010 published on January 1, 2011.

Public Procurement Oversight Authority (PPOA) (Second Edition November 2012), Public Procurement and Disposal General Manual (PPDGM)

ABOUT THE AUTHOR

Evans Vidija Sagwa is a Lecturer at the Technical University of Kenya and a former Chairman of the Department of Labor and Workplace Studies. He teaches courses in management to certificate, diploma, higher diploma, undergraduate and post graduate students in addition to supervision of projects and theses. He is an adjunct Lecturer at the University of Nairobi. Dr. Sagwa has previously worked in the private sector and has for several years has been involved in consultancy and training assignments for various organizations. He is a Full Member of the Institute of Human Resource Management (IHRM) in Kenya, has authored a book *Fundamentals of Development and their Applications to Kenya* and co-authored another book entitled Principles and Practice of Management.

www.ingramcontent.com/pod-product-compliance
Lightning Source LLC
Chambersburg PA
CBHW071819200526
45169CB00018B/471